972.91   c.1

CASTRO.
    FIDEL CASTRO.

1986   25.00   3-87

8 9   1991
  1   1

Alameda Free Library
Alameda, California

NOTHING CAN STOP
THE COURSE OF HISTORY

Fidel Castro: Nothing Can Stop the Course of History

Interview by Jeffrey M. Elliot and Mervyn M. Dymally

C.1

PATHFINDER PRESS

New York   London   Sydney

972.91
CASTRO

To E. Victor Maafo
*A treasured friend and colleague
at North Carolina Central University, for his wisdom
and wit, caring and passion,
and support and encouragement*
— J.M.E.

A volume containing the interview granted by Fidel Castro to Jeffrey M. Elliot and Mervyn M. Dymally was published in 1985 by Editora Politica (Havana, Cuba), under the title *Nada podra detener la marcha de la historia*. Excerpts from this interview also appeared in the August 1985 issue of *Playboy* magazine.

Copyright © 1986 by Jeffrey M. Elliot and Mervyn M. Dymally
All rights reserved

Library of Congress Catalog Card Number 86-061524
ISBN cloth 0-87348-660-9; ISBN paper 0-87348-661-7
Manufactured in the United States of America
First edition, 1986

Pathfinder Press
410 West Street, New York, New York 10014
Distributors:
Africa, Europe, and the Middle East:
  Pathfinder Press, 47 The Cut, London SE1 8LL England
Asia, Australia, and the Pacific:
  Pathfinder Press, P.O. Box 37, Leichhardt, Sydney, NSW 2040 Australia
Canada:
  DEC Book Distribution, 229 College St., Toronto, Ontario M5T 1R4 Canada
New Zealand:
  Pilot Books, Box 8730, Auckland, New Zealand

Photographs by Gianfranco Gorgoni

Contents

Preface

Whatever one may think about him and the Cuba that he symbolizes, Fidel Castro has long been an object of fascination. Praised or damned, what he says and does is remarked on around the world. The interview published here goes a long way toward explaining why. The background to how I became involved with it is also a fascinating story.

In the summer of 1984, the Reverend Jesse Jackson and I traveled to Cuba to meet with Fidel Castro. As a result of that visit, the Cuban government agreed to the release of twenty-two U.S. citizens who had been imprisoned either for drug trafficking or illegal entry into Cuba, and several Cuban prisoners.

I returned to Havana the following December. Part of my trip was a humanitarian mission — two of my constituents from Los Angeles, Cubans by birth, sought my assistance in their efforts to reunite their family. We succeeded, and when I left Cuba I brought with me their young daughter and her grandmother. I also brought with me Fidel Castro's agreement to participate in what was to become one of the most significant interviews the Cuban president has ever granted — the longest in over twenty years for a U.S. audience.

Obtaining Castro's agreement for the interview was a goal I had set for myself before leaving for Havana. Earlier that year, Dr. Jeffrey M. Elliot had interviewed me — along with twenty-four other prominent Black leaders — for his new book, *Black Voices in American Politics* (Harcourt Brace Jovanovich, 1986). Out of that interview a close friendship had developed. I enlisted Dr. Elliot's participation in the project of arranging the interview with Castro.

Our enthusiasm for this project was to be matched by Fidel Castro's. The Cuban president's only condition was that the interview cover not only U.S.-Cuban relations, but the state of the world.

It was an extraordinary experience — exhilarating, but exhausting. Our original intention was to conduct the interview over a three-day period (Friday-Sunday). The sharpening congressional debate on the fate of the MX missile meant I could not stay in Cuba very long. I knew I would have to return to cast my vote against that measure. Likewise, Dr. Elliot also had pressing commitments. As it turned out, the interview was to span a nine-day period.

Our first day in Havana, Friday, March 22, 1985, was to typify the entire, arduous experience of the interview. On arrival, we were taken to our hotel and told to wait in the suite for a call from the president. Having arrived in Cuba at the hour set by Cuban officials, we expected the phone call at any minute. We were still waiting, ten hours later. We later learned that Nicaraguan President Daniel Ortega had arrived the same day and had met with Castro.

The next day we awoke certain that the interview would begin early in the day, since we were scheduled to leave Cuba the following evening. At 11:00 p.m. that night, the call finally came — Castro would see us. This was, however, not to be part of the interview, but rather a get-acquainted session.

As it turned out, this was to be a session where Castro interviewed us. Through an interpreter, he greeted us genially — and then went on to pose sharp questions about the project, pointedly and repeatedly chastising, by name, a series of U.S. journalists for their lack of integrity and their general ignorance. After much discussion, Castro finally agreed to do the interview, but not until Sunday, the following day.

Needless to say, it wasn't until Monday, at 11:00 p.m., that the interview finally began. Immediately following that session, I flew to Washington in order to vote against the MX missile. On Thursday, I flew back to Havana, and we resumed the interview with Castro.

Each night at approximately 11:00 p.m., a government van would arrive at our hotel and take us to the Presidential Palace, where we would speak forthrightly with the president until dawn. Adding to the complexity of the interview, Castro spoke entirely in Spanish and we were required to work through an interpreter. We left each session completely fatigued.

When we left Havana, we took with us twenty-five hours of tapes, undoubtedly the longest and most wide-ranging interview ever conducted with Castro. In it, Castro speaks directly to the people of the United States on questions of vital importance to citizens of both our countries.

The interview — and this book — spans dozens of topics: U.S.-Cuban relations, the Reagan administration's foreign policy, the New International Economic Order, unity and disunity in Latin America, Cuba's relations with Africa, the events in Afghanistan, right-wing dictatorships, the arms race, and the effects of the U.S. economic blockade on Cuba. It also includes many personal insights about Castro himself — his character, his relations with the Cuban people, his views of Cuba itself. The result was an interview of historic importance.

That's the background; that's the story of this volume. I am delighted, of course, to have had the opportunity to co-author this work with my foreign affairs advisor, Dr. Jeffrey M. Elliot.

> — Rep. Mervyn M. Dymally
> Washington, D.C.
> May 1986

The United States has never wanted to accept the existence of the Cuban revolution or the establishment of a social system that is different from its own.

Jeffrey M. Elliot: In recent years, there have been fierce differences between our two nations. What do you see as the chief reasons for the deep divisions which divide our two countries?

Fidel Castro: In my view, the United States is responsible for the present situation. It has never wanted to accept the existence of the Cuban revolution or the establishment of a social system that is different from its own. The United States never cared about the existence of dishonest, tyrannical governments in this country — governments that killed thousands of people and stole huge sums of money. It never cared about this country's poverty, ignorance, unsanitary conditions, or the lack of schools, hospitals, and medical services. It never really cared about the unemployment, racial discrimination, and enormous social problems in our country. It never cared. These were never reasons for concern or for blockades against Cuba.

Then, when a revolution took place that put an end to those problems, the United States set about trying to destroy the revolution in Cuba. That's really the origin of some of the problems. It is also what, ever since the very beginning, has brought about all kinds of measures — from the most insulting and slanderous campaigns against Cuba, to plans of subversion, the organization of armed bands, acts of sabotage that killed many people, mercenary invasions, the cancellation of the sugar quota that Cuba had had for 100 years, the economic blockade, the policy of isolation, plans of aggression, and assassination attempts against the leaders of our revolution. It's an endless list of U.S. actions against our country. Plus there is the maintenance of a military base by force, against the will of our people. That is what lies behind these divisions.

Naturally, this has caused great indignation among our people and their strong repudiation of all those policies. However, we haven't attempted to blockade the United States or engaged in other acts of aggression against that country. No, it has been the United States which has done so against Cuba. If the United States doesn't change those policies, I don't see how these differences can be overcome. I state categorically that we aren't the ones responsible for the current situation.

Mervyn M. Dymally: To what degree, if any, has President Reagan exacerbated the situation?

Fidel Castro: Reagan has clearly exacerbated the situation. He has resorted to a policy of continual threats against our country, which has forced us to make enormous efforts to strengthen our defenses. He has also intensified the blockade.

Reagan has compounded the problem in numerous ways. First, he put an end to U.S. travel to Cuba, which had been reestablished for some years. He has also incessantly and tenaciously endeavored to place obstacles in the way of Cuba's economic and trade operations. Clearly, many U.S. officials are engaged in compiling information on our economic and trade operations with the Western world, in order to try to keep us from selling our products, to block our nickel sales to Western nations, and to try to prevent loans to Cuba and even the rescheduling of the debt. Each time we reschedule our debt with various bankers, the United States draws up documents and sends them to all the governments and banks.

I remember when, over a year ago, the representatives of the creditor governments met here. They were all given a document that attacked Cuba's arguments for rescheduling the debt. We had a copy of that document, too, and, in our discussions with the bankers, I showed it to them and asked, "Isn't it a shame that the United States is attempting to block all this?"

That is, the Reagan administration has implemented a constant policy. Not only does the U.S. blockade ban all trade between the United States and Cuba, it even bans trade in medicine. This is shameful! We can't get a single aspirin from the United States; it is legally forbidden. Medicines that may save many human lives are forbidden. No medical equipment can be exported from the United States to Cuba. Trade is also prohibited in both directions. The United States has also expanded its boycott throughout the world, as part of its policy of unceasing harassment — shameful and infamous harassment — against Cuba's economic operations. The only reason it doesn't interfere in our trade with other socialist countries is because it can't. And that's the truth.

Mervyn M. Dymally: Are you willing to meet with President Reagan, without a prearranged agenda, to discuss ways in which to improve the relationship between the United States and Cuba?

Fidel Castro: In the first place, you should ask the president of the United States that. I don't want it to be said that I am proposing a meeting with Reagan. However, if you want to know my opinion: I don't think it's very probable. But, if the United States government were to propose such a meeting, we wouldn't raise any obstacles.

Mervyn M. Dymally: What if the United States Congress or, more specifically, the Congressional Black Caucus, extended you an invitation to visit the United States? Would you accept such an offer?

Fidel Castro: I have very good relations with the Congressional Black Caucus. I know many of its members, and any invitation from them or any opportunity to meet with them, either in Cuba or the United States, would be an honor for me.

Still, I would first have to know the position of the U.S. government, because a visit to the United States requires a visa from the U.S. government. If that were possible, indeed, if that could lead to a broader meeting with U.S. legislators, then I think I have the arguments with which to talk, discuss, and debate — either with a group of congressmen or the entire U.S. Congress.

If this condition were met, I think I could go. There are many things to talk about that would be useful for the members of Congress to hear. And I could answer all of their questions. However, all of this is hypothetical. I don't think it can be done unless President Reagan agrees.

Jeffrey M. Elliot: When you work in your office late at night and you're by yourself, with your own thoughts, and reflect on the status of U.S.-Cuban relations, do you ever wonder whether this conflict can ever be resolved?

Fidel Castro: First of all, I have so many more pressing, and more feasible, things to think about, that I have little time to reflect on that topic. However, I concede that yours is a good question and, furthermore, I like the way you've asked it.

I do think so — that some day it can come to an end — but it will take time. There's the example of China. Eventually, the day came when the United States became more realistic. I won't say it was entirely opportunistic — that it sought only to exploit the differences that emerged between China and the Soviet Union. Rather, it became more realistic, as it did when it called a halt to the Vietnam butchery — that absurd war, a discrediting war for the United States. It went on for thirty years, since before Dien Bien Phu, with the direct and indirect participation of the U.S. Thirty years had to elapse, millions of tons of bombs, millions of victims, tens of thousands of U.S. citizens killed, hundreds of thousands of U.S. citizens wounded, many of them traumatized, with serious psychological problems, before they put an end to that war.

We certainly wouldn't want these things to occur in Latin America. I'm hopeful that one day the United States will adopt a more realistic attitude toward its relations with the Latin American peoples. Of course, such changes in views almost never come about as a result of reasoning, fair ideas, or in-depth analysis. Unfortunately, they usually occur when problems or crises arise. That's why one talks, explains, and reasons — trying to make it understood that there are policies that are wrong, that have been wrong for many years, and that such policies lead to crises.

I'm convinced of the unavoidable crisis of U.S. policy toward Latin America. It's built on the old idea of the United States acting as the proprietor of the countries of this hemisphere, in contempt for its peoples. This contempt is at times evident in speeches, in the simple things, in anecdotes, stories, and the toasts that are made. You can see it in the contacts with Latin American leaders and in the existence of a kind of catalog of anecdotes and historical facts. They scornfully consider that flattering words and blandishments dedicated to a given leader or a country can obliterate the cancer of poverty, underdevelopment, and socioeconomic and medical needs which have accumulated in this hemisphere. But this cancer cannot be cured by amenities or by speeches full of adjectives about "brilliant statesmen" or by kind words. I have the impression that when Columbus, Cortés, Pizarro, and the European conquistadors reached this continent, they treated the Indians in almost the same manner, and with the same philosophy — which did not exclude the philosophy of bartering mirrors and other trinkets for gold. I think that is the conception of the U.S.

I notice it, I feel it — not when they talk with me, because none of those U.S. visitors can talk like that with me. Besides, the visitors I receive are usually a different type of person. But when I look at the official policy of the most outstanding figures of the United States — of the presidents of the U.S. in their relations with Latin America — it's impossible not to sense the contempt, the derision they feel for the peoples of Latin America. They look down on the Latin American peoples as a strange mixture of proud and ignorant Spaniards, uneducated black Africans, and backward Indians. They view us as a strange and uncommon mixture of people who warrant no consideration or respect whatsoever. Some day that policy — the policy of intervening in all the Latin American countries, establishing guidelines, dictating what type of government should be elected, and determining those social changes that can and cannot be made — will give out and result in a crisis. I really believe that moment is drawing nearer — that policy will give out and result in a crisis in the not-too-distant future.

The United States has been fortunate that, up to now, these problems have arisen in small, isolated countries like Cuba, Grenada, and Nicaragua. It can still afford to speak of invasions, interventions, and solutions based on force, as occurred in 1965 against another small Caribbean country — the Dominican Republic. But, when the U.S. is faced with similar problems everywhere in the southern hemisphere — in any one of the large- or medium-sized countries in South America — it won't be able to solve them through intervention, dirty wars, or invasions, because that would be catastrophic.

No one can guarantee that revolutionary changes will take place in South America, but neither can anyone guarantee that they won't take place at any time in one or more important countries. It seems to me that if one objectively examines the economic and social situation in these countries, there can't be the slightest doubt that an explosive situation exists. If an urgent solution is not found for these problems, more than one revolution will take place in South America when the U.S. least expects it — and it won't be able to blame anyone for generating or promoting these revolutions.

Since I can picture very clearly what will happen, I have been raising these problems, insisting on these problems, with all the people from the U.S. I meet. Maybe my effort will prove useful and make at least some people in the U.S. reason things out.

Perhaps, when the United States was about to embark upon the Vietnam War — as it enthusiastically did — if someone had persuaded the people as to what was to happen there, he'd have done a great service to the people of the U.S. For example, it is said that if the *New York Times* had published the story it had concerning the planned Playa Girón (Bay of Pigs) invasion, it would have done Kennedy a great service and would have prevented that mistake. We are now doing exactly that with respect to Central America. Seeing how the United States government — I can't say the people there, because 72 percent of them oppose military intervention in Central America — moves with similar enthusiasm toward intervention in Central America, we are not doing the people of the United States a bad turn when we warn them, and insist on warning them, about the consequences.

I don't think we're doing a bad service to the people of the United States when we insist that a truly volatile situation is developing in Latin America. When that happens — as it undoubtedly will if certain problems aren't urgently solved — the United States will then be faced with serious problems which it won't be able to tackle with the concepts, ideas, and methods it has historically used in dealing with the peoples of Latin America.

Let me give you an example: in the United States, there was great contempt, scorn, and disdain for the Cuban people. Cuba was the most secure, docile, and best indoctrinated colony of the United States. The Cuban people were considered to have no desire to work and no patriotic feelings and to be perfectly indoctrinated in anticommunism and antisocialism, totally impervious to a revolution by virtue of U.S. ideology and culture. I believe that, at present, the United States would have no reason to underestimate the Cuban people. During these past twenty-six years, Cuba has shown what a Latin American people is capable of doing; that this mixture of Spaniards, Africans, and Indians has far greater political, organizational, and combat capacity than the United States ever imagined.

We are no different and no better than the Central Americans, the South Americans, or the rest of the Latin Americans. No, I consider that they have the same potential qualities we had, and perhaps even more. The day came when we rebelled and resolved — despite the risks and at all costs — to follow our own independent path and carry out the social changes we have undertaken. Those problems can't be solved by force or by arms.

I honestly believe that the United States will have to adapt to this reality. It will have to change its conceptions. But it does not necessarily have to wait for social and political cataclysms to treat Latin American countries with more respect and less contempt. When that day comes, when that conceptual change occurs, the foundations will start to be laid for establishing relations of understanding and respect — even of friendship — regardless of the divergent ideologies and social systems in Cuba and the United States.

Jeffrey M. Elliot: All great leaders must be dreamers, but they must also be pragmatists. Ultimately, peace and understanding between our two countries will require that both sides meet, talk, reason, and, yes, compromise. After all, each nation believes strongly in the moral legitimacy of its own stance. Is Cuba willing or able, at this critical juncture in U.S.-Cuban relations, to compromise, perhaps not on fundamental issues, but on those issues which might pave the way for improved relations? In other words, is compromise possible on your part?

Fidel Castro: Your question is one I should have asked myself: On what important issues could we reach an agreement — when faced with the present U.S. view regarding Latin American and world problems, because we most certainly belong to the world; when we see that the economic relations that are developing between the United States and Latin America are really unbearable; when the most elementary numbers and figures show that the hemisphere is being pillaged? I can prove it; and I'm going to prove it to you.

In 1984, due to the deterioration in the terms of trade — that is, due to the way the prices of Latin American exports have dropped and the way the prices of imports from the industrialized countries have increased when compared to 1980 — the United States delivered 22 percent fewer products for the same amount of exports than four years previously. In that way, it deprived these countries of $20 billion. Through excessive interest, it deprived them of $10 billion. And through the flight of capital, of hard currency, it deprived them of an additional $10 billion. Moreover, through the overvaluation of the dollar, it lent them, for example, a dollar worth 100, and is now charging them a dollar worth l35 in return. It's as if you lent me a kilogram of gold, but expect me to repay 1.35 kilograms, plus the interest spread. I made a very conservative estimate, and, in 1984 alone, this plunder amounted to about $5 billion. In these four categories, the United States is, at present, arbitrarily and abusively depriving Latin America of $45 billion every year.

Who's responsible for such high interest rates? The monetarist policy of the United States. Who's responsible for the flight of capital? For the most part, that same U.S. policy of high interest rates and all the other factors mentioned, which generate runaway inflation in the economies of the Latin American countries.

Who's responsible for the 22 percent decrease in the purchasing power of Latin America's exports? Here, I'm not going to blame just the United States; it's the entire industrialized capitalist world, which has, in practice, imposed a law — namely, the law of unequal exchange and of the growing deterioration of the terms of trade.

If you examine those relations from 1950 to 1985, you'll

see a declining — a constantly declining — trend in the purchasing power of Third World products. That is, the price of the products we import from the industrialized world is forever increasing, while the purchasing power of the products we Third World countries export is forever decreasing. We are sold ever more expensive equipment — produced with wages of $1,000 or more, with large profits for the companies — so they can buy products manufactured with wages of $70 or $80. That's the historical trend. And that's the U.S.'s trend. The United States must bear an important share of the responsibility, as an industrialized country dominant in the Western economy.

If, in order to be a friend of the United States, we must remain silent and never pose these problems, then we cannot be friends. If the United States believes it is entitled to intervene in Grenada, Santo Domingo, and Nicaragua — to wage a dirty war in the latter — then we cannot be friends. If the United States feels it is entitled to overthrow the Arbenz government in Guatemala and the Allende government in Chile, or to promote the overthrow of Goulart in Brazil, then we cannot be friends. If, furthermore, the United States declares, as it did a while ago, that the Western world should be thankful to Pinochet for overthrowing the constitutional government elected by the people in Chile, thankful for the overthrow and death of Allende, for the rivers of blood shed since, and for the untold suffering it entailed for the people there, what should we do? Keep our mouths shut and not speak about those things? Not denounce those things, so as to have good relations with the United States? There are economic, political, and moral problems — all very serious — and we feel it is our duty to denounce them before the United Nations, before all international organizations everywhere.

Can we then compromise on these things? I think that there may be topics, different types of questions on which compromises can be made. But on these really basic questions which involve the reality we are witnessing, concessions are impossible. And let me tell you, there must be a change in conceptions for these things to disappear. How? Who can guarantee that?

You were telling me that each country strongly defends the things it believes in. The problem, however, is to determine which country is strongly defending objective or subjective things, just or unjust causes. Right? I understand this problem. But it would be necessary to identify those compromises that both we and the United States could make. For instance, mutual respect between the two countries is possible; there could be normal relations of peaceful coexistence between the two states. Trade relations could exist. Cultural exchanges could take place. Still, there must be a will to identify all those points on which this would be possible. One would really have to sit down and think about it.

However, given the aforementioned things — which, in my view, are very important and are matters of principle — this will be difficult. It's not a question of a feeling of hostility toward the United States, much less toward the people of the United States. No such feeling of hostility exists. This can be seen in the things I've said. They are not inspired by hostility. They are motivated by an interest in creating a better understanding and preventing serious problems both for the countries of Latin America and for the people of the United States themselves.

It's not the individual who makes history but the people.

Mervyn M. Dymally: People in the United States know Fidel Castro, the revolutionary; Fidel Castro, the Cuban leader. However, they know very little, if anything, about Fidel Castro, the man. Who is Fidel Castro? What motivates him?

Fidel Castro: That's too broad a question. It would almost be necessary to write a book to answer all that, my motivations. [*Laughter*] I'll try to answer.

First, let me state those things that do not motivate me. Material goods do not motivate me. Money does not motivate me. The lust for glory, fame, and prestige does not motivate me. I really think ideas motivate me.

Men do not remain the same from birth to death. I think that man is also like a river, constantly flowing. Someone once said that no one bathes twice in the same river; man's life is also like that. Ever since you're born, when you're practically a small animal, you act by instinct. Then you begin to have the first emotional reactions, the first moral notions, the first knowledge about the world, about people. You get an education; you learn how to read and write, and enrich your knowledge about the world around you. I think it's a process of constant evolution, even of changes in man, once he starts to acquire ideas, principles, ethics, sentiments. Many of these things you learn at home, at school from your teachers. They are ideas, notions, values, that are instilled in man — and many of them are extremely important.

At some point, man begins to have political ideas, to have his own ideas. The ideas resulting from his analysis, his reflection, his awareness, aren't necessarily those instilled in him. They may not even be the ones taught to him.

Actually, no one instilled my political ideas in me; I came by them gradually. Naturally, I absorbed various influences from existing ideas, opinions, and conceptions. But the option was entirely my own — the result of meditation, reflection, observation of reality, and an analysis of what other men did and thought. They were really my own ideas. I came by them as a result of certain conclusions: a conviction that transcended my social milieu, my class origins, my education, everything I read in the press, saw in the movies, everywhere. I think that's of great importance in man's motivation. He reaches certain conclusions, certain ideas, that spur him to struggle, because he's really convinced of what he's doing.

Naturally, I can assess my own ideas, from the time I started having political ideas, revolutionary ideas, up to the present. These ideas have developed gradually. The values I started off with in this struggle have also developed. My commitment to, as well as my interest in, these ideas has grown over the years. I believe that the struggle itself — in the circumstances in which we've had to wage it — has also been an incentive. It is something to which you are devoted, and you feel more convinced and more committed with each passing year. I think that personal selflessness can grow with each passing year. The spirit of sacrifice can grow. At the same time, the subjective, personal things become less important. You reach such a degree of identification with what you're doing that you gradually relinquish personal pride, vanity, all of those things that, in one way or another, exist in all men.

If not, the contrary may occur. You grow less and less interested in things. Subjective elements exert a greater influence. You may become conceited and cherish the idea that you're more knowledgeable than others, that you're indispensable, irreplaceable, and you become infatuated with what you are and what you do.

All of that may happen. Fortunately, the latter is not true in my case. I think that's partly due to the fact that I've been on guard against all those things. Maybe I've developed a philosophy about man's relative importance, about the relative value of individuals, the conviction that it's not the individual who makes history but the people. Nobody can lay claim to the merits of an entire people — millions of people who work every day, contribute their efforts every day, produce, and defend the revolution. I hold the deep-rooted conviction that it's mere vanity to strive for personal glory. This, to a certain extent, may explain my attitude. There is a thought, an idea, a phrase by José Martí that left a deep and unforgettable impression in me. It taught me, it pleased me, and since then, I have always had it in mind: "All the glory of the world fits into a kernel of corn."

It's really comforting to feel that one may have managed to elude those risks. Is there some method to achieve that victory over yourself? I don't think there are any infallible techniques. Human beings are very complex. I've always found it useful to be on guard — to be critical, rigorous, demanding of myself — and to try to be honest with myself. You must be committed, dedicated to what you're doing, enthusiastic about your efforts, and convinced of the worth of what you're doing.

Jeffrey M. Elliot: Most men, at some point in their lives, question themselves, doubt themselves, wonder whether they can meet the challenges they've set for themselves. In your case, most people view you as supremely confident, strong willed, determined. Have you ever questioned yourself, doubted yourself, wondered whether you could realize your objectives?

Fidel Castro: Really, to the question of whether I've ever had doubts about what I'm doing — Let's start from the moment I took up political, revolutionary activities. I must say, in all frankness, that I can't recall ever having had doubts or a lack of confidence. I've never had them. That may be good, or it may be bad. If what you're doing is objectively correct, then not having doubts is good. But if what you're doing is objectively bad, then not having doubts is bad.

I try to explain to myself why I've never had doubts. Ever since I conceived my first ideas and set myself a line of work and struggle, I have always persevered. I must admit that, at a given moment, even pride might have influenced my attitude toward difficulties, toward obstacles. And if the truth be known, I encountered very great obstacles. But once I had a clear sense of what I had to do — and I had great confidence in those ideas — throughout my life I have been encouraged by the fact that those premises have been borne out. In order to understand this, you must consider that when the struggle against Batista started, all I had were ideas; I didn't have a cent, a single weapon, or an organization. Then I began to work on the basis of certain premises.

I don't believe that success is, in any sense, a measure of whether you're right or not. People often say: he was right; the facts have proved it. And yet, I'm convinced that we could have been defeated. If that had occurred, it wouldn't have proven that we were wrong. Throughout this struggle, there have been times when chance alone allowed us to survive. There were times when our group could have been wiped out — more than once. If that had occurred, it wouldn't have meant that we weren't right or that what we were doing wasn't correct. That didn't happen; quite the contrary. There are men who are right, independently of their times and circumstances. Sometimes chance may make someone look as if he weren't right, but other men in other times and circumstances — and perhaps with greater luck — show that the one who wasn't successful was, in fact, correct.

This has taught me that success isn't proof of the correctness of the undertaking. The success achieved isn't what persuades me that what we were doing was what should have been done. I have a lot of evidence and proof that our ideas were correct, even if we hadn't triumphed. We faced very great difficulties, very difficult moments. One was after the twenty-sixth of July 1953. We'd worked hard on a plan to seize the Moncada Garrison, but accidental factors prevented our success. Then came the time in prison, beginning again, the trip to Cuba in 1956 and the conditions under which we made it, and seeing our forces once again dispersed and disorganized. Those were difficult trials.

I remember — and this could have been a moment of great doubt — when we were attacked by surprise and our forces were totally dispersed. This, in fact, was accidental. I'm not referring to the causes that can lead to difficulties, but rather to ideas, a state of mind. I was left with two comrades — three men and two rifles. It was a hard day, a very hard day. The planes caught us by surprise, and it was a miracle that we weren't all wiped out. We were walking through a field of sugarcane that had just begun to grow. We didn't know what the range of visibility of a reconnaissance plane was at 500 or 800 meters. Later on, I learned that, at that distance and at a certain altitude, you could even see a bird on the ground. It was broad daylight. We'd been surrounded. The area was crawling with soldiers. Then, all of a sudden, fighter planes appeared and attacked us directly. In the midst of heavy strafing, we moved into a cane field that was taller and covered ourselves with dry leaves. We expected enemy soldiers to arrive at any minute. The reconnaissance plane kept circling overhead.

As a result of many days of tension and exertion, I became extremely sleepy. I was sure I was going to fall asleep, regardless of how hard I tried not to. I remembered the time that same army had captured me asleep, at dawn, with no one on guard, with the soldiers' rifles aimed at my chest. This was some days after the attack on Moncada. I couldn't forget that moment, but I just couldn't stay awake. I was going to fall asleep. I wasn't carrying a pistol but a rifle with a telescopic sight, impossible to manipulate if I were caught sleeping. I lay down on my side, placed the barrel of the gun under my chin and the butt between my legs, undid the safety latch, and fell fast asleep.

Several hours went by. I think I slept for about five hours. I'd fallen asleep around midday. When I woke up, the sun was setting. No one knows if the soldiers came nearby to see the results of the strafing and to look for bodies. Undoubtedly, that was the hardest day.

After that, I could have concluded two things: it's impossible to continue this struggle under such circumstances; we've got to get out of the country and organize another expedition. But at that moment, I told myself: "Well, we've had a setback; we've been dispersed. But the idea was correct. We've got to press on and reach the mountains." At that moment, I had only two rifles with which to continue the struggle. Still, I decided to continue, convinced that the conception was correct, that the idea was just.

Days later, I made contact with some of the other comrades who'd been dispersed. All told, we had seven rifles. We pressed on, and when we reached the wooded area of the Sierra Maestra, I said, "Now, we've won the war." At that time, there were twelve of us. Some of those who survived, recalling the moment years later, even joked about that apparent excess of optimism. I was convinced of what I had said.

We've come through some very hard trials, some very difficult days, but we've prevailed. That particular experience explains — can help to explain — why we never had any doubts about what we were doing. You can analyze whether you did things well, better, or worse; whether you made mistakes or should have done one thing or another at a given moment. But that has nothing to do with the essential idea, the essential aim, the correct line you're following. Up to this very moment, I've never had that kind of doubt, and I hope I never will. Day by day, I become more convinced of what I'm doing. Now, I don't think there's much room for having doubts.

Still, it's quite another thing to have a critical, self-critical spirit, asking yourself if you're doing your best, if you've done things the best possible way, if each decision was best, if you've been sufficiently demanding of yourself. You have to keep analyzing what you've done at each turn. You have to be rigorous, hard on yourself, and never feel complacent about the things you've done.

Sometimes on reviewing the different stages of the revolution, I've said: "I'm amazed by the inexperience with which we began to do things, the ignorance with which we set out along this road." It's now possible, for example, to analyze the entire process since the triumph of the revolution, and, when we compare the experience we had then with the experience we have now, it's rather amazing. This happened in the war, too. We can compare what we knew when we began it with the experience we had gained when it ended, and it surprises us to see how ignorant we were when we started out. But learning how to make a social revolution was a longer and more difficult proposition than waging a war. We had some basic ideas about what we had to do — ideas that were fair and correct, no doubt — but no experience and not even a precedent to indicate how to carry it out under the specific circumstances of a country such as ours.

During those early years, as may happen in any victorious revolutionary process, we had a somewhat iconoclastic spirit. Although we were totally unaware of it, we were a bit know-it-all and arrogant. While a revolutionary must always be arrogant in the face of the enemy, we were sometimes arrogant with friends, too. There was a tendency to magnify our own achievements in comparison with other revolutionary processes. We felt capable of interpreting the doctrines and postulates of Marxism and socialism more accurately and faithfully than others. That led to an insufficient understanding of the historic merits of other revolutionary parties and countries and of the enormous obstacles they'd had to overcome. It also led to an underestimation of their experience. Our critical appraisals often weren't sufficiently serene, reflective, or profound. This may even have had something to do with certain idealistic tendencies and with expressions of a phenomenon that is very difficult to eradicate from this world: exaggerated national pride.

Today, while we're certainly happy about our work and the contribution Cuba has made to revolutionary practice and theory, we have a broader view and a deeper appreciation of the enormous contributions made by other revolutionary processes.

I honestly believe — and this can, indeed, be cause for legitimate pride — that a long time ago we stopped being know-it-all, arrogant, idealistic, and even chauvinistic — which we may have been in the early years of the revolution. I think we now have a better understanding of both the historic processes and the men and women who are side by side with us carrying out the revolution in Cuba. We possess a greater understanding not only of their virtues, but also of their limitations and faults.

My admiration for what man is capable of doing — for his enormous potential for sacrifice, solidarity, and nobility — as well as my understanding of his human limitations have grown. I believe that many years of having great responsibilities and authority can corrupt a man, but I also believe they can improve him. I've tried to be less and less jealous of those powers; to share them more and more with others; to regard myself as ever less indispensable; and, with every passing year of my life, to view with greater clarity the relative value of individuals and the immense merit of the legion of anonymous heroes who constitute the people. In short, I've never had any doubts, but neither have I been completely pleased.

Jeffrey M. Elliot: In what sense haven't you been completely pleased? Aren't you satisfied with the results you've achieved?

Fidel Castro: Maybe I'm a bit of a perfectionist. I always try to set the highest possible goal. If you're doing a job — you've called together a group of comrades to analyze a certain topic — after it's over, you think about all the arguments that were presented. After attending a congress where you've had to take the floor many times, as in the recent women's congress or the sessions of the National Assembly of People's Power, where many topics are broached and discussed, you run over each point and always wonder if you could have gone a bit deeper, used more and better arguments. You may even wonder if you were rude in the debate, if the way in which you replied to a comrade may have hurt his feelings. I'm usually very careful about this. Whenever I have to criticize a comrade, the first thing I do is to try to protect him, to keep the criticism from being destructive, so it won't demoralize him, and so that — while serving as an example for others — it deepens his commitment and encourages him. Then, you stop to think about whether you did it with the utmost care, whether you've fully achieved your purpose. You stop to think about whether you included all the elements in a speech, all of the data, and presented them in the best possible order. The same thing happens to me after every interview. [*Smiles*]

Something else often happens to me when I deliver a speech. Sometimes I have to speak at length, because it's my job to try to persuade, to argue — at times, to insist — and to reiterate. Generally when I'm finished, I'm not pleased. Later on, I see the transcripts — this is in the case of speeches that weren't written ahead of time — and I often feel better about them then as opposed to just after the speech.

Sometimes, when I've had an interview such as this one, I've had the impression that I wasn't as orderly in handling the topics as I might have wished. Then, when I read the transcripts, I appreciate the effort that was made. I even see, when it's a long interview, that as time goes by, I tend to be more fluent, clearer in my presentation of ideas.

I've given you these examples because you constantly have to analyze every word you say — every single word — and how you said it, at the moment you said it. You should always analyze what you do. That's why I say you're never quite satisfied. I think such an attitude is useful, it's positive. It's like when an athlete does something wrong and says to himself: "That was wrong. I have to do better next time." I think this happens to a lot of people. There are great writers — famous writers — to whom this happens. They're never satisfied. According to Stefan Zweig, Balzac corrected the proofs of his novels a thousand and one times, up to the very last minute, even though he desperately needed to be paid for his books. If you apply that approach of never being quite satisfied with everything you do, you'll have a formula that, I think, politicians should follow.

At least you have to be on guard against self-complacency and conceit. Unfortunately, some people are always content. They consider that what they've done is perfect. This doesn't help, especially in the case of men with responsibilities. Conceit, pretentiousness, intolerance, and inflexibility tend to grow when men have authority and power. I've even noticed this in some comrades. I've seen it: sometimes, when a person is given some authority, shortly after he starts to behave differently. Finally, though I'm never satisfied with what I do, I'm nevertheless very confident in and certain of what I intend to say or do.

Mervyn M. Dymally: What qualities make for a great leader? Do you believe you have those qualities?

Fidel Castro: I think I have the qualities to do what I'm doing.

Now, what makes a great leader? What does the concept of a great leader imply? Moses was a great leader; Christ was a great leader — here, I'm referring to spiritual leaders. I think Mohammed was a great leader. They were personalities in history who are known as leaders, because each had a doctrine, founded a doctrine, and was followed by multitudes. Even when they started out, they were backed by a few. Christ, it's said, was followed by twelve apostles at first, then by millions of believers. He was a spiritual leader, as was Mohammed. They were religious leaders — but leaders, nonetheless.

I have an idea of what a leader is. Ho Chi Minh was a great leader. And, for me of course, the one with the most extraordinary qualities as a political and revolutionary leader was Lenin. Lincoln was a leader, a really great leader. There were many leaders in the history of Latin America. Without a doubt, Bolívar was a great leader, both politically and militarily. Throughout the history of Latin America, there have been many leaders who have led their countries under difficult conditions. In this century, Roosevelt was a leader, that's beyond question. I'm referring to the Roosevelt of the New Deal.

There have been many religious and political leaders. History is full of leaders. Wherever a human community has existed, a leader has emerged. The times determine what is required of them. Certain qualities are needed at one time, others at another. In the Napoleonic era, it seems that it was military qualities that were required: battles, prestige, glory. The French revolution itself had many outstanding leaders. Under certain circumstances, the important thing was the ability to wage war; in others, it was the ability to think, to reason; in still others, the gift of expression, to make speeches, to convince others; in yet others, the capacity for action; and, in still others, the ability to organize. In short, you can't describe a leader with any one model.

Now, I'm going to talk about a current leader: Jesse Jackson. He certainly has the qualities of a leader. His ability to communicate, deep convictions, ethics, and courage in the milieu in which he lives and works — the United States is a very difficult one — all bear witness to his leadership qualities.

Each epoch, each society, each historical moment demands certain qualities. It's possible that leadership qualities in the future will differ from those needed in times of revolutionary struggle: the imagination and audacity that were required at a given moment. Perhaps some other time will demand cooler-headed, less intuitive, more methodical people — another type of man, the right man to lead society in a different phase of its development. But a certain amount of creative spirit and imagination will always be needed. Regardless of how much a society develops, there will always be room for improvement and change.

The qualities required at one moment are not necessarily the ones needed at another. We're talking about serious leaders, aren't we? We're not talking about demagogues or electioneering politicians, because sometimes they have to be good demagogues, have good publicity, a good public image, and even be good looking, to get votes — a lot of votes. Then they've got to have television and special advisers. Advertising specialists can make leaders. That's not what I had in mind. I'm talking about men who are capable of generating ideas, of inspiring confidence, of directing a process, of leading a nation in difficult times. That's what I'm referring to. I think the characteristics vary greatly from one situation to another, from one time to another, from one people to another. There are many.

If you ask, "What about the qualities of a revolutionary leader?" I could go into it a little deeper. I might have a little more to say about that. I think a revolutionary leader needs to have a lot of conviction, passion, for what he's doing. He also needs to have great confidence in the people. He must be tenacious and cool-headed and have a sense of responsibility and of identification with what he's doing and with the people. He also needs some training, some clear ideas. Well, there you have a few elements.

I'd like to add one more qualification to the concept of a revolutionary leader. He should also have a great sense of human solidarity, great respect for the people. He should view the people not as an instrument, but as a protagonist — a real protagonist — the subject and hero of the struggle. Now, I don't mean to suggest that those qualities are technically indispensable for leading a process of change. There may be a leader who has all of the other qualities and yet views the people as an instrument, an object, rather than as the main protagonist and real hero. That could happen. It might. That would be more of a moral assessment than an evaluation of the intrinsic characteristics that a leader needs.

Other men have proved capable of leading regressive processes in history. Take Hitler: he was a leader, at least technically. He had some of the characteristics required for being a leader — but, of course, not a revolutionary one. He was a fascist leader, a reactionary leader, who communicated with the masses and stirred people's passions, their resentment, their hatred. He appealed to the lower instincts of man and rallied multitudes. Morally, he was no leader at all.

I'm thinking, rather, of revolutionary leaders; about what is required of a leader who is to make a positive mark on history. I mentioned the German case, the demagogue, as an exception — an example of an individual who, under certain circumstances and using certain methods, can rally people behind a bad cause. I'd prefer that type of demagogue be excluded from the concept of a leader.

There's something else I want to say about this. I think that many people have leadership qualities. It's a mistake, a serious mistake, to think that these qualities are rare or infrequent. I'm convinced of this. For a leader to emerge, the only thing needed is the need for a leader.

In revolutions, leaders emerge. The masses produce an infinite number of people with great qualities.

If we talk about the independence struggles in Latin America, for example, dozens of political and military leaders emerged. If we talk about the French revolution, a great many leaders emerged from the masses, people who no one had heard of the day before. They were brilliant, capable, excellent orators, such as Danton and Mirabeau; great pamphleteers, such as Marat; and rigorous, methodical military chiefs, such as Robespierre — all ephemeral, in keeping with the dynamic and complex nature of the process itself. Great leaders also emerged in the thirteen colonies and led their people to independence. Many people have leadership qualities. Circumstances determine which of them becomes more prominent than others. These circumstances are often fortuitous; chance is a factor. For instance, in the history of the independence struggles, those who organized a struggle often died and then others with great capabilities emerged. That's why I maintain that all that's needed for leaders to emerge is that there be no leaders.

I recall our experience during the war. After our initial victories, we had a column of 80 to 100 men. You had to urge each of the men in charge, every day, to insist on discipline, vigilance, and the maintenance of a permanent state of alert, stressing that there be no carelessness. Later, when you chose some of the comrades who excelled and assigned them the responsibility of commanding a new column, they then established discipline and saw to every detail. If you assigned them to an area of action, they really excelled. That is, when they were given important missions and assumed responsibility, many people showed what they could do. It was a small group, and many outstanding leaders came from it. This means that a man needs responsibility to develop his potential.

Let me give you some examples. Indira Gandhi was a great leader. She knew the problems of India, the psychology of her people, and the characteristics of the country. She did an excellent job. What was the determining factor, however? Her family ties with Nehru. That was the factor which gave her her opportunity. Right now, the same is true of Rajiv Gandhi. I believe he's doing his job — which isn't an easy one in that huge, complex country — with a great sense of responsibility. In his case, too, the opportunity arose because of family ties.

What I mean is, it can't be assumed that leadership qualities are exceptional. I think it was Aristotle who said that man was a political animal. Political genius is more widespread than artistic genius.

There's something else. I'm convinced of this, and it's easy to prove: the emergence of leaders is determined by the historic moment and objective conditions. Let me cite several examples. If Lincoln had lived today, he might be a simple farmer in the United States, and nobody would have heard of him. It was the times in which he lived, the society in which he lived, that made a Lincoln possible. If George Washington had been born fifty years after independence, he might have been unknown; the same holds true if he had lived fifty years previous to it. The conditions at that historic moment were what made a Washington possible. Let's take Napoleon, a great military leader. What would have been his lot if he had been born fifty years earlier? He might never have left his small Corsica. If Lenin, with all his exceptional ability, had been born at the beginning of the past century, he would have been unknown in history.

I believe that human beings, all human beings, have a great capacity for political leadership. What must have happened on countless occasions is that the possibilities for developing those abilities did not arise, because the person lived in a different era, under different circumstances.

I maintain that, wherever there are 1,000 cadres, there are many potential leaders.

Take my case, for example. If I hadn't been able to learn to read and write, what role could I have played in the history of my country, in the revolution? Where I was born, out of hundreds of kids, my brothers and sisters and I were the only ones who had a chance to study beyond the first few grades. How many more people were there among those hundreds of kids, with the same or better qualities for doing what I did, if only they had been given the opportunity to study? The first thing that eliminates many talented and capable people is the social factor; they simply didn't have the least opportunity to study.

One of the 100 best poems in the Spanish language tells of how often genius lies dormant in one's innermost soul, awaiting a voice that would call out, "Arise and go!" This is true; I believe this deeply. That is why I believe that the qualities for leadership are not exceptional; they are to be found among the people.

The Cuban revolution itself is the best proof of this. In this country, for example, there were hundreds — thousands — of prominent people: political leaders, ministers, deputies, senators, and mayors. There was an enormous number of political and military figures who were well known and recognized in that social milieu. Then the revolution came along and not a single one remained in public office. Virtually everyone who took charge of running the country later on — who became political leaders, military leaders, administrative leaders, and cadres at all levels — was completely unknown. Five, three, or two years before the revolution, the people knew few, if any, of the farmers, workers, professionals, or students — the humble citizens who later shouldered the responsibilities of leadership. No, in order to be absolutely precise, I should say that half a dozen comrades from the old Communist Party were known throughout the country, but none of them held public office.

The entire leadership of Cuban society was replaced with people who came from the masses. Around 200,000 new professionals have graduated from our universities since the triumph of the revolution: men and women who are engineers, doctors, economists, and professors, with much more theoretical training. And millions of people have obtained incomparable levels of political training.

On one occasion, when a comrade [Camilo Cienfuegos] who had had an outstanding record in the war died — he disappeared in a plane accident — I spoke about it on television and said, "There are many Camilos among the people; many men like him will emerge from the people." He'd been living in California at the time we were in Mexico, and he came and joined our ranks. He participated in the landing and was one of the men in the small group that survived and continued the struggle. What did I first think of him? At that time, we were all going hungry. He had a tremendous appetite, and, if any food was left when the others finished, he was always the first one to ask for seconds, although he did so in a very disciplined manner. The only thing I remember about him at that time was his voracious appetite. No one could have imagined the extraordinary military, political, and revolutionary qualities he possessed — which were brought out only after the fighting, after the military operations began.

The same was true of Che Guevara. Che — we called him that because he was Argentine — came as a doctor. Nobody then could have imagined his talents as a soldier, as a revolutionary thinker, his remarkable integrity. Che left Argentina immediately after medical school. He arrived in Guatemala, witnessed the overthrow of Arbenz, and then moved to Mexico, where I met him. What I said earlier was again borne out; if he hadn't run into us in Mexico, or if he'd been killed in the difficult early moments, only a few of us would have known him. The Che we all know wouldn't have existed, for we wouldn't have known who he really was.

What does this mean? There are potential values everywhere that only need an opportunity to develop. This is also true of military figures. If it weren't for the circumstances that gave rise to a great world conflagration, few would have heard of Eisenhower, Patton, MacArthur, or any of the others who achieved renown in the United States during the last world war. Without that war, who would have known of the existence of de Gaulle?

There is a fabulous potential capacity in the human mind and heart. It's said that people use only 5 or 6 percent of their mental capacity — there are scientists who are doing research on this. No one can imagine the kind of computer man has in his head.

Why am I saying this? I've noticed, especially in the West, that there's a great tendency to associate historical events with individuals. It's the old theory that individuals make history. There's also a tendency in the West to view the leader of any Third World country as a chieftain. There's a certain stereotype: leader equals chieftain.

I'm amazed that, in the West, where you suppose that there are cultured societies and that people think, there's such a strong tendency to associate historical events with individuals and to magnify the role of the individual. I can see it myself, in such phrases as: "Castro's Cuba," "Castro did this," "Castro undid that." Almost everything in this country is attributed to Castro, Castro's doing, Castro's perversities. That type of mentality abounds in the West; unfortunately, it's quite widespread. It seems to me to be an erroneous approach to historical and political events.

Mervyn M. Dymally: In what ways, if any, have you grown as a leader since assuming power?

Fidel Castro: I've already told you. It makes me shiver to think about my ignorance at the time the revolution triumphed; it amazes me. I've gained a lot of experience, knowledge, and maturity. I'm sure of this. I began by saying that we have freed ourselves of subjectivism and touchiness. If you ask me if we've improved, I would say, "Yes, I think so. We've improved in every way, including the human aspect." I told you earlier that in the beginning we tended to be know-it-all, arrogant, and less understanding of the problems of others and even of their mistakes.

Jeffrey M. Elliot: As president, you're forced to live your life under the microscope of public scrutiny. Do you find it difficult to live life in a goldfish bowl?

Fidel Castro: Actually, I never think about that. I'm never even aware of it. There may be something that explains this. My activities are almost never reported in the press. I may be doing a lot of things for fifteen days; yet none of it comes out in the papers. You may have noted that almost every country has what is called an executive press office. Everything the president or prime minister does throughout the day is published in the papers and reported on television and radio. In a sense, ivory towers or fishbowls are built around them. I haven't created a fishbowl for myself. I visit factories, schools, and the various provinces and towns. True, I visited them more often in the past, but that's because I had more time then. As the country has become more institutionalized and organized, there is less chance, less time for moving around everywhere. But there's never been any protocol or welcoming ceremonies, as is customary for leaders in many countries.

If there's a public rally — for instance, on July 26, which is an important occasion — it is publicly announced. I go to the rally and usually speak. But all my life — throughout the past twenty-six years — I've gone everywhere without ceremony, without protocol, without publicity. The comrades at the places I visit often argue that the people should be told that I was there. Sometimes I give in and let a public announcement be made, since they feel that this is a source of motivation and is useful for their work.

I go anywhere. I visit the universities and other schools. I meet with many people, both Cubans and foreigners, and my work becomes a natural thing. But sometimes crowds gather where I go. How long since I last ate at a restaurant? Why? A new Chinese restaurant recently opened in Old Havana, which is being restored. It's small and cozy, in an old building. For some time, I've wanted to go to the restaurant. But if I go, a crowd may gather. I can't conceive of sitting there quietly, eating on the second floor, while a large crowd of people stand in the street, waiting to see me. Still, these are minor inconveniences, which go with the job.

I have ways of getting around this. If I want a rest, if I want to relax, I go to the sea. I go to a small cay out there — anywhere. I haven't created a fishbowl for myself, nor have I let myself be placed in a fishbowl. There isn't any fishbowl. Sometimes I'd like to go to the beach; I loved it when I was a student. Of course, if I go there, crowds gather. I only go there in passing, when I'm taking a visitor on a tour of those places. All right, I have to resign myself. Whenever I want to go to the sea, I go far out, on the shelf, near the cays. There are some marvelous bottoms, fish, and coral reefs, and I've grown accustomed to those places. When I was a student, no one ever thought of ocean scuba diving as a sport. There were all sorts of stories about sharks, too. I'm convinced that scuba diving is one of the most wonderful forms of recreation. I deprive myself of some things, but not too many, and I'm really accustomed to it.

I've never had that fishbowl feeling of being viewed through a microscope, or living in an ivory tower. I've really not felt it.

If it's ever worthwhile to devote time to a public presentation of the economic problems of Latin America and the Third World, the time is now.

Jeffrey M. Elliot: In recent months, you've granted several lengthy interviews to some of the most well-known journalists in the United States. For the first time, in nearly two decades, the American people have had an opportunity to see and hear you expound on the state of U.S.-Cuban relations. Why did you grant these interviews? What did you hope to accomplish?

Fidel Castro: It's true that I've granted several interviews in the past few months. In general, I'm plagued with a great many requests for television, radio, newspaper, and magazine interviews. I can't tell you how many; it must be between 150 and 200 a year. It would be physically impossible for me to grant them all. In general, my work load doesn't slack off, and, as a rule, I refuse to grant interviews; they're very time consuming. As I told you in our first contact, I like to take things seriously. In an interview, I like to answer questions personally and not entrust the task to someone else or answer some questions in writing. Furthermore, it always implies a certain amount of tension: what is said, what is published, how everything is construed.

Now then, this year I've entrusted certain tasks to other comrades, who have taken some of the daily work off my shoulders. Thus, I've been able to grant several interviews — not just to the U.S. press, but to the European press, as well. For example, I've granted interviews to the Madrid daily, *El País*; the Spanish news agency; Swedish television; the Mexican daily *Excelsior* and, of course, a larger number of interviews to the U.S. press, because it's been pressing me the most lately.

I thought it would be useful to do this now. I'm not trying to launch a publicity campaign, much less improve my image. I'm not running for office in the United States. [*Smiles*] Rather, I'm doing this because this is a special time in our area and even in the international situation. It seemed to me that these contacts with the press would help to publicize our views and our thoughts about the situation. For example, there's been a tense situation in Central America, and I believe there is a really critical situation in Latin America, both economically and socially. Moreover, there is great international concern over the problems related to the arms race and to the dangers of a war. At the same time there are conflicts in southern Africa. If these problems are better understood, some contribution may be made to their solution.

This decision was spurred by several events in the latter part of 1984. Jesse Jackson's visit to Cuba was one of the important events that led to these intensified relations and public contacts with the U.S. press. Extensive talks were held at that time — even a press conference — in which various problems were examined, including migration problems between our two countries and the issue of those "ineligible" for taking up residence in the United States, as some who had left via Mariel were considered.

On that occasion, I publicly explained my answer to Jackson, expressing our readiness to discuss the problem even before the 1984 elections, if both political parties agreed. Indeed, in April 1984, the U.S. government had expressed its readiness to discuss this problem, including various immigration questions.

Let me put it more clearly: the United States had several times raised the issue of sending back to Cuba those citizens of Cuban origin who were considered ineligible for residence in the United States. Ever since the last few months of the Carter administration, this problem had been posed in terms of discussing both the question of the "ineligibles" and migratory relations. When the Reagan administration took office, it proposed only one topic for discussion — namely, the return of the "ineligibles" —

rather than both questions, which was our position. Finally, in April 1984, the Reagan administration agreed to discuss both issues. However, the election was close at hand, and we were concerned that this might become an issue in the electoral race. We didn't consider that advisable. That's why, when Jackson raised the issue, we explained the background to him and expressed our willingness to discuss the matter prior to the election, if both parties agreed. Within seventy-two hours, the Reagan administration expressed its readiness to hold immediate discussions. A few days later, through Jackson, we asked the Democratic candidate, Walter Mondale, what he thought, and he also agreed. On the strength of this, the talks began in New York.

This process was interrupted in August by an unexpected RS-71 spy flight. The plane flew over the middle of the island, from west to east, and returned along the same route. I feel that this was an unnecessary, ill-timed action. Similar flights hadn't occurred for many months — since the end of the previous year. Moreover, it was totally unnecessary, because the United States has satellite surveillance and flights around the island — all it needs for detecting and photographing any of the facilities and movements it may be interested in, without violating Cuban airspace. That incident led to the interruption of the talks, until it was made clear to us that the flight wasn't intended as a means of exerting pressure on or humiliating Cuba.

In October, it was agreed to renew the talks and a date was set for after the election. The fact that the United States showed interest in discussing this issue after the election allayed the suspicion that it might be just an electoral ploy.

This also coincided with several other events, including President Reagan's statements after the election reiterating his readiness to engage in international negotiations and to seek some sort of agreement or understanding between the Soviet Union and the United States. Moreover, in Angola, U.S. and Angolan representatives were holding talks and examining formulas for the solution of the conflicts and tensions in southern Africa, a negotiating process in which the Angolans have acted in close coordination with us. The problems of Central America and the Contadora countries' efforts were also considered, and various possibilities for a solution could be foreseen.

These factors should be considered together with the development of the talks in New York between the United States and Cuba — talks which, as I have said on other occasions, were serious, flexible, and respectful. Progress was made, despite the complexity of the topics, and mutually satisfactory agreements were reached in a relatively short period of time.

We considered this to be positive. The possibility of solving complex problems through talks had been demonstrated in practice. Taking all the other things into account, we found it possible to hope for a more flexible, more realistic policy by the United States. Furthermore, this coincided with the Gromyko-Shultz meeting in Geneva and their later statements. This seemed to create a framework, a more favorable environment, for the search for solutions to complex international problems. Some U.S. legislators — Alexander, Leach (a Republican), and Leland — and a large group of businessmen and scientists visited Cuba, and I had some extensive talks with them concerning our views on all those problems. Therefore, we thought it would be relatively useful — to avoid confusion over Cuba's positions, among other things — to have these contacts with the press in the U.S. and other countries, in order to present our viewpoints clearly.

We were well aware of the fact that a serious socioeconomic crisis — an explosive, controversial crisis — was taking place in Latin America. It seemed to me that United States and world public opinion as a whole wasn't aware of that situation, which could jeopardize the entire process of democratic openings which had begun in

Argentina and extended to Uruguay and Brazil. Serious political and social upheavals might take place in South America. I felt it useful to pose this problem — which I believe requires attention and must be solved soon — in meetings with the press. I also thought it advisable to provide world public opinion — including U.S. public opinion — with elements for making a judgment, with information, and to let it hear these views in a truly constructive spirit. If we hadn't felt this constructive spirit, if we'd taken an irresponsible attitude concerning these problems, we would have remained silent and not addressed them publicly. But that attitude runs contrary to our views, because we hold that those problems can be solved before serious conflicts erupt in the Latin American region — conflicts which would, in one way or another, affect all countries in the hemisphere.

So, all those factors influenced my efforts to create increased awareness about the situation, including an attempt to persuade world public opinion, and even U.S. public opinion, of the fact that a solution could be found to these problems. That was my conviction — and I uphold it — that such a solution can be found. It seemed absurd for the United States to embark on an interventionist policy in Central America, which is part of a hemisphere that, I believe, is becoming a powder keg. Its doing so helps neither the Central American countries, Latin America, nor the United States itself. And, based on my conviction that the United States was pursuing the wrong policy — that everyone would benefit if that trend were halted — and in order to broach all these other problems, I made a special effort to present our views in the interviews I'd been requested to give. I was interviewed by CBS's Dan Rather, the *Washington Post*, PBS, the daily *El País*, the Spanish EFE news agency, the daily *Excelsior*, and other press organs. I sometimes found myself in an embarrassing situation, when two or three important U.S. TV networks requested interviews at the same time. What should I do?

Who should I see first?

At the same time, several renowned writers suggested that I write a book — a history of the revolution. Many editors have also expressed interest in this. I simply availed myself of these possibilities to convey my views.

The examination of these problems has been a constant in all my statements. My delay in seeing you was caused by my interview with the Mexican daily *Excelsior* — a very long interview, which lasted many hours, and which forced me to give it a lot of time. By the way, it came out today, with a front-page headline — the first in a series of three articles on the economic problems of Latin America and the Third World. I have always covered that in my interviews. I think that these things are very important and that, if it's ever worthwhile and useful to devote time to a public presentation of these problems, the time is now. That's my explanation. I've spoken at great length on this matter, but I wanted to tell you, frankly, why I did this.

Jeffrey M. Elliot: As you've stated, you've granted several extended interviews. However, the nature of television, almost by definition, dictates a condensation of such lengthy discussions. Have you seen any of those interviews? Did they accurately reflect your views?

Fidel Castro: I believe the PBS interview was a serious one, on interesting, complex topics. It was a long interview in which, naturally, I agreed to answer any questions they wanted to ask, and the journalist made broad use of that prerogative and kept me before the cameras for four hours.

I knew that that interview was for a small audience. I saw several segments of it, and I'd say that some basic things on serious topics were raised, especially with regard to the economic situation and Latin America's foreign debt. I've received reports that many people wrote in for video cassettes of the program. At the same time, as usual, we filmed the interview. Since the work is shared, both parties have rights to it. Those who do the interview always have priority, but, naturally, we also have the right to publish a complete version in Cuba. It's important for our people to have all of these elements in order to form accurate judgments. I don't get paid nor have I ever requested a single cent for this work. I also sent cassettes to nearly all of the other Latin American countries and to some of our important regional leaders, so they could hear our views. But, of course, as you indicated, television's possibilities for spreading detailed and complete reporting on the topic are, by definition, very limited.

After PBS, there was the interview with Dan Rather. I don't think very important problems were discussed in that interview. It was much more anecdotal, containing my personal views of Reagan and other topics of that nature, which may be of interest to a certain audience. Some of his questions — such as the one about an alleged Soviet submarine base in Cuba — really astonished me, since they showed a basic lack of information about what is going on in Cuba and in the rest of the world.

That interview, too, took time. Little television time was devoted to it, as was only logical. It was very anecdotal. It ran fifteen minutes, plus five minutes the day before on another topic — namely, why I hadn't attended Chernenko's funeral. Rather has a lot of material left over, which he may use at any time. I'm perfectly aware that, sometimes, you make a great effort and put a lot of time into something, and then they take up anecdotal rather than essential matters. That's why, as I told you the other day, if you want to express your views in depth, you have to develop them and present them in a pamphlet or a book, so they reach all interested readers.

We sent the interview with the Spanish news agency throughout Latin America, to all the major media. We printed it in full in pamphlet form, and it has been distributed widely in Latin America. I was interested in having people know these views. Maybe a part of the *Excelsior* interview, the part on the Latin American debt, will be printed as a pamphlet and spread widely not only in Latin America but throughout all Third World Countries. I'm planning to send these views to many political leaders, since I believe it's a very important and serious problem, and therefore very important for it to be known — not only by scholars, economists, and the public, but also by the political leaders. Often, due to their numerous day-to-day obligations or for other reasons, the political leaders are the least informed about these matters.

Mervyn M. Dymally: How do you respond to the charge, as voiced by the U.S. State Department, that your recent conciliatory statements are, by and large, a public relations ploy?

Fidel Castro: Public relations as such would be meaningless. I have just talked at length about that. I think the effort I have made over the past several months, in the middle of my many occupations, is worthwhile and can be justified only by a constructive purpose — to contribute, at least modestly, to overcoming certain problems.

Ideas are of great importance; if problems are not clearly understood, they cannot be solved. The effort I've made was aimed — as I told you — at producing an awareness of serious problems of the present and how, in our opinion, they could be solved. It's a real shame that the State Department holds this view, which actually reflects confusion, superficiality in analysis, and ignorance about the methods and style I've maintained throughout my life. Instead of criticizing these actions, it would befit the State Department to express its gratitude for this effort to call attention to the problems I've dealt with in these interviews.

What would be the value — I ask myself — of such a public relations campaign? On other occasions, the interviewers have responded favorably to our discussions and expressed appreciation for the care which we've shown. I'm aware that this interview that I promised you — considering the persuasive arguments you put forth regarding the U.S. public — will take a lot of time and that some topics may be outdated by the time it is published, though I hope not many of them. Still, I think it's very important. The fact is, however, you requested the interview — not me.

Cuba has stood sentinel against the drug traffic in the Caribbean — as a matter of self-respect. We have the most outstanding results of any nation in this hemisphere in the struggle against the production of, trafficking in, and use of drugs.

Jeffrey M. Elliot: Earlier, you mentioned the Chernenko funeral. As you know, your absence at the Chernenko funeral attracted a lot of press coverage. Speculation ran high as to why you failed to attend. Why, in fact, did you not attend Chernenko's funeral? Did your absence signal, as has been reported, a rift in Cuban-Soviet relations?

Fidel Castro: Look, I was present at Brezhnev's funeral. I was present at Andropov's funeral. I've attended the last two Soviet party congresses — that is, almost all the most important state occasions that have taken place in the Soviet Union. One must bear in mind that the distance between Cuba and the Soviet Union is great; one can get to the Soviet Union quickly from Europe, Africa, India, and the Middle East. The other socialist countries are only two hours away from Moscow, sometimes less, and the leaders can get there quickly. We, on the other hand, must make a very long trip to get to the Soviet Union.

So, there were two events which I did not attend. First, the Council for Mutual Economic Assistance summit meeting — which I have never attended but nonetheless gave rise to much speculation. Second, the death of Chernenko — a person for whom I had great esteem, whom I'd known for some time, and who was very friendly toward Cuba. Chernenko's funeral occurred at a time when I had an enormous amount of work. Despite my interest in meeting Gorbachev and other world political personalities who would be present at the funeral, on the day of Chernenko's death, we had just concluded a women's congress, to which I had devoted several days of intense work.

I'm going to tell you something else. On the very night when the first news arrived, I was meeting with several delegations of women from Latin America who were scheduled to leave the following day. I spent the entire night meeting with those delegations: first, as a group, and then in interviews with individual delegations. I was supposed to have had two days of rest, and yet by morning, I had not had a minute's sleep. That same morning, at dawn, the Soviet ambassador asked me for an interview. It was obvious that it was the official communication of the death of the leader of the USSR. I was in my office and, on the way home, I dropped by the embassy specifically to offer my condolences, talk a while with him, and find out about the funeral arrangements. At that time, we had not yet decided on the composition of the delegation to the funeral. We calculated the time and realized that the delegation would have to leave for Moscow at 5:00 p.m. in order to arrive the following day and attend the funeral. For the previous several days, I had had practically no rest.

Let me say something else, since you force me to. Between the end of the Congress of the Federation of Cuban Women, where I delivered the closing address — that was Friday evening — and 8:00 a.m. Sunday morning, I worked for forty-two consecutive hours on certain materials that had to be finished without any possible delay. I rested a few hours, after which came the activities I just mentioned. It occasionally happens that way under certain circumstances; fortunately, not always. Since I also had numerous commitments with foreign visitors in the following days, and I was worried about keeping them waiting — and you are exceptional witnesses to the fact that I don't begrudge my time or energy in attending visitors, regardless of their political rank — I decided to ask Raúl [Castro] to represent me at the funeral. I made the decision, bearing in mind that Raúl is not only second secretary of the party and first vice president of the Council of State and of the government, but also that he has been personally acquainted with Gorbachev for several years and had friendly relations with him that date back to a visit he had made to the Soviet Union.

In short, it didn't seem reasonable for me to preside over the delegation. It involved too great a physical and mental exertion, as well as leaving aside pressing affairs in order to fulfill a formal obligation. That isn't the only way to show affection, appreciation, and respect for a friend.

I can tell you, in all frankness, that our relations with the Soviet Union are excellent — better than ever. And precisely because of the confidence they have in us and we have in them, I knew they'd understand. I would have liked to go, not only because of the Soviet people, Chernenko, and the opportunity to greet Gorbachev, but also because on such occasions a great many leaders come from Africa and Asia — many friends — and it would have been an opportunity to greet and talk with them. But under the circumstances, it was not logical, not rational, to do so. I'm struck by the importance that my absence was given. I couldn't have imagined that the things I do or don't do could have such an impact in the United States — that they would warrant so much attention, so many articles, so much publicity.

Mervyn M. Dymally: In your view, why do so many Americans have such a negative view of Cuba and Castro? What explains the deep negative feelings which exist?

Fidel Castro: In the first place, it's not so much a negative view toward Cuba and Castro, but fundamentally an antisocialist, antirevolutionary, and anticommunist view. For more than 100 years — in the United States, Europe, and elsewhere — this anticommunist feeling has been drilled into the masses, into the people by every possible means. This anticommunist indoctrination begins practically when the child is born. The same thing used to happen in our country, precisely as in the United States — a permanent campaign in all of the newspapers, magazines, books, films, television, radio, and even children's cartoons. The purpose is clear: to create the most hostile ideas and prejudices against socialism. I'm referring, of course, to a socialist revolution, not just to the much-used and often-abused word, *socialism*, which so many bourgeois parties have currently taken up as something elegant in an attempt to dress up old-fashioned capitalism in new clothes. In other words, that's what's at the root of those anti-Cuban and anti-Castro feelings.

I'd like to elaborate a bit on this idea. There's no doubt that, for twenty-six years, the mass media have been manipulated and used in this campaign against Cuba to spread all sorts of lies about our country. I'm not afraid to accept responsibility for all we've done in these twenty-six years. I'm not afraid to discuss any problem, any topic, and debate any issue concerning the history of the revolution. But, really, a study could be made on how much space, how much paper, how much press has been directed against Cuba. Only recently a film was made in the United States: it recalls the worst moments of the cold war and McCarthyism. It's based on a fictional invasion of the United States by the Soviets, Nicaraguans, Afghans, and Cubans in order to kill U.S. students, women, and children. I haven't seen the film, but I've heard about it. You can well imagine what sort of propaganda is being made in the United States against those who do not resign themselves to the capitalist system.

This shows, moreover, that the people of the United States are really some of the worst-informed people in the world, despite their huge technological resources and mass media. And I say this with sorrow: they are one of the least politically educated and worst-informed peoples on the realities of the Third World, Asia, Africa, and Latin America. All this is actually at the root of the anti-Cuba, anti-Castro feelings. The anti-Castro part doesn't worry me as much as the anti-Cuba part.

Now, I'd also like to say that, in turn, there is a broad minority of people in the United States who think, who have a high cultural and political level, who do know

what's happening in the world. But they are not representative of the average citizen. Furthermore, I know for a fact
that there are many U.S. citizens who are not taken in by
those phobias, by those prejudices, by those anti-Cuba
feelings — because I've had the opportunity to talk to
many of them and appreciate their political level and ra-
tionality. They don't have any of those feelings. At least I
see decency and good faith in many of those who are ill-in-
formed.

I talk to religious people from the U.S., from the Protes-
tant churches, the Catholic church, intellectuals, scientists,
researchers, doctors, and, of course, many representatives
of the people of the United States — like yourselves, or the
delegation that came with Jackson. I don't get the impression that they're full of prejudice, of anti-Cuba sentiment.
Quite the opposite, they strike me as people who are better
prepared than anyone to understand us, because they are
aware of many of the injustices which exist within the
United States. So, not everyone is so misguided. Moreover, one can't forget what Lincoln said: "You can fool
some of the people all of the time, but you can't fool all of
the people all of the time."

On the other hand, I want to remind you of something.
Twenty years ago terrible things were said about China,
about Mao Tse-tung, about Chinese communism, about
the red threat, about the yellow threat, and the inconceivable threats that China posed. The press used to say the
worst things about China every day. However, that's no
longer the case. The press is no longer full of such insults
against the Chinese government and the People's Republic
of China. Quite the opposite, there are excellent diplomatic relations, investments, and increasing trade. And this
process did not start with today's China but with the China
of Mao Tse-tung — at the time of the Cultural Revolution,
at the time when an extreme form of communism was
preached and applied in China.

They established diplomatic relations. Economic relations began and now there are exchanges of cultural and scientific delegations and also visits by prominent people. Even Reagan had the pleasure of visiting China, climbing the famous wall, viewing historical sites, and enjoying Chinese cooking. Military delegations visit China, and China is even supplied with weapons and technology. Look how everything has changed.

And why? Can you tell me why? Now, there are even two kinds of communists: good communists and bad communists. Unquestionably, we've been classified among the bad communists, and I am the prototype of the bad communist. Well, Mao Tse-tung was also included in this category for a long time. Of course, if changing the concept of a bad communist to that of a good communist implies that we stop denouncing the things we deem incorrect, that we stop assisting the causes we deem just, that we break our ties of friendship with the Soviets, and that we become anti-Soviet in order to become good communists, acceptable to and applauded by the U.S., then we will never become good communists.

If one day the United States changes its policy toward Cuba and public opinion has the chance to learn the truth, it will have to be on the basis of its ability to realize that neither the Cuban people nor Castro are opportunists, turncoats, people who can be bought. If the United States should some day become our friend, and is able to appreciate the revolution and those who have fought to make it possible, then this friendship would have to be based on respect and on an honorable concept of our country. As I told the legislators who were here recently, no one respects those he buys.

Mervyn M. Dymally: Reagan administration officials have testified before Congress that the government has concrete evidence of a Cuban-Colombian drug connection. Is Cuba actively involved in drug trafficking? If not, how do you explain such charges?

Fidel Castro: One of the Ten Commandments says: "Thou shalt not bear false witness against thy neighbor." The Reagan administration should constantly be reminded of this commandment. Besides, I believe that the people of the U.S. and the U.S. Congress deserve more respect.

It's absolutely impossible for the U.S. government to have a single shred of evidence of this kind. These are, in my view, dirty, infamous methods, a totally dishonest way of conducting foreign policy. If we stick to facts, during the last twenty-six years, Cuba's record in this regard has been spotless. In our country, prior to the revolution, drugs were used, sold, and produced. The very first thing the revolution did was to eradicate that problem. Strict measures were taken to destroy marijuana fields and to strongly punish all forms of drug production and trafficking. Since the victory of the revolution, no drugs have been brought into Cuba, nor has any money been made from drugs coming from anywhere else.

Moreover, during the twenty-six years since the revolution, I haven't heard of a single case of any official who was ever involved in drug trafficking — not one. I ask if the same could be said in the United States, or if it could be said in any other Latin American or Caribbean country or in the rest of the Western world.

Between 1974 and 1985 alone, 306 drug smugglers were caught in Cuba: 91 from the United States and 215 from other countries, including 118 Colombians, at a steady rate every year throughout this period. We have seized 599,166 pounds of marijuana — over 280 tons, part of which came from Jamaica — and 1,024 pounds of cocaine, around a half a ton. We have seized twenty-five planes — twenty-four of them from the United States — and fifty-six vessels — thirty-seven of them from the United States, twelve from Colombia, and the rest under other flags.

We have all the data, case by case, about the strict sanctions imposed. On many occasions — for humanitarian purposes — U.S. senators and representatives have approached us expressing concern about the welfare of U.S. citizens arrested in Cuba on drug charges and even suggesting that we release them. As you know, in the United States, congressmen are constantly harassed by requests about anything and everything from the voters in their districts and states. They attempt to do everything possible to accommodate those requests. It's a tradition. The relatives of these U.S. citizens always try to help them. It's logical. We released the last ones — about twenty, if I'm not mistaken — in the middle of last year, at the time of Jackson's visit. But, a number of foreigners keep coming to Cuba for this purpose, month after month.

These convicted drug smugglers never carried out any actions against Cuba. They know that drugs are neither produced nor sold here. They are apprehended by the Cuban authorities when their planes land in our territory for one reason or another. They usually land only when they have engine trouble, become lost, or run out of gas. Or they are caught when their boats, for the same reasons, enter our territorial waters. Naturally, they try to avoid landing in Cuba or making any sort of stop on our coasts, because they have considerable experience with the consequences and the strict measures taken in our country. Keep in mind, Cuba has an east-west axis in the Caribbean and is over 1,000 kilometers long but only 50 kilometers wide in some places. It's easy to cross the island in a matter of minutes and to be under international jurisdiction again. Our radar frequently detects airborne targets approaching or departing our territory. U.S. spy planes do this almost every day, even without entering our airspace; occasionally, they do it with sophisticated aircraft that fly at an altitude of 30 kilometers, at 3,000 kilometers per hour. I imagine that those planes aren't carrying drugs.

Small civilian aircraft frequently penetrate our airspace. They don't pay our interceptors the slightest attention. Having to decide whether or not to fire on an unarmed civilian aircraft poses a serious, tragic dilemma. There's no way you can be sure who's in it. It's not like an automobile, which can be stopped, identified, and searched. The passengers may be drug smugglers, but they may also be off course or trying to save fuel by taking a shorter route. They may be families, journalists, businessmen, or adventurers — of which there are many in the United States — who are afraid to land and be arrested in Cuba.

There's a lot of propaganda against Cuba in the United States. They know they won't be fired upon, so they laugh at the order to land. Had we fired in every case, hundreds of planes would have been downed. Of course, this can't be tolerated indefinitely. That's why we have asked the U.S. government to do what it can to halt these illegal civilian flights over Cuba's sovereign territory. I understand perfectly that the U.S. government has little, if any, control over aircraft used by drug smugglers. But if it can guarantee that the other aircraft which normally operate out of airports in the southern part of the United States don't engage in such violations, the risk of shooting down a civilian aircraft with innocent people on board will be reduced. Of course, if Cuba decided to take drastic measures against civilian aircraft which violate the airspace of our country and refuse to obey the orders of the interceptors, that responsibility would have to be shared by the governments of Cuba and the United States.

Cuba is the place most feared by drug smugglers. Although our country has been blockaded by the U.S. and has no obligation to cooperate with the United States on this or any other problem, Cuba has stood sentinel against the drug traffic in the Caribbean — as a matter of self-respect, a simple question of prestige and moral rectitude. Is it fair that the treatment we receive in exchange for this is the infamous accusation that Cuba is involved in the drug trade?

Furthermore, we've behaved similarly toward other problems. In the early years of the revolution, Cuba was offered millions of dollars for one simple thing: the number that was going to be drawn in the lottery each week. Some people even said, "We're not asking that you give us a specific number. All we ask is that you draw it a week earlier and send it to us." All the illegal lotteries from Miami to New York were run on the Cuban lottery, whose winning number was announced over the radio each week. Not only did we categorically turn down such offers, but, in time, in line with our revolutionary program, we even did away with the lottery.

There's something else: more than once, Cuba has been offered fabulous amounts of money if we would cooperate in drug deals. Although we are blockaded by the United States, we have never accepted a single drug deal. Therefore, I say it is infamous to attempt to link Cuba to drug deals. I can state categorically that we have never received a single cent from drug trafficking. We have the cleanest record and most outstanding results of any nation in this hemisphere in the struggle against the production of, trafficking in, and use of drugs. It is truly shameful that the United States — the largest drug market in the world — is making such an accusation against Cuba. We know that the United States is growing more and more marijuana, and that it is already being produced in most states in that country. It wouldn't be surprising if the United States wound up producing synthetic cocaine.

What is truly immoral is to
force people to go hungry;
to live in poverty; to live
in the worst material,
educational, cultural, and
health conditions in order
to spend a trillion dollars
on weapons and military
activities every year. That
is what is really
immoral — not the
cancellation of the debt.

Jeffrey M. Elliot: In recent interviews, you've spoken at length about the critical importance of the economic crisis which presently grips Latin America. In your view, why hasn't the international community responded to the problem with greater urgency?

Fidel Castro: For several reasons. I suppose that when you say the "international community," you mean the industrialized community, the developed countries — and mainly the Western countries, which are the ones that have the closest economic relations with the Latin American and Caribbean countries.

First, because of their indifference to and lack of real concern about the economic, social, and human tragedy which the Third World countries are currently experiencing.

Second, because of their lack of awareness, responsibility, and foresight with regard to the serious political problems that exist, especially those that will arise in the short and medium term. It is possible that when the problems reach a crisis stage — and there will be a crisis — they will become aware of and begin to be concerned about those problems.

Third, because of selfishness. They enjoy a privileged economic relationship with the Third World countries. They buy cheap raw materials, cheap exotic products for which they pay less and less, and they sell ever more expensive manufactured products.

Fourth, because they have become accustomed to a system of privileges, which they aren't at all interested in renouncing.

In 1984, for example, Latin America transferred economic resources worth more than $70 billion to the industrialized countries. These included interest on the debt and profits, $37.3 billion, and deterioration in the terms of trade, $20 billion. What does this mean? That if Latin America, for a certain number of its exported products could purchase $100 worth of products from the developed countries in 1980, that same number of exported products in 1984 acquired only $78.30 worth. If trade or exports worth around $95 billion is considered, the loss under this heading amounts to slightly over $20 billion. That is, Latin America has transferred merchandise, economic values, worth $20 billion without receiving anything in the exchange.

In addition to remittances under these two headings, we must add — and this is a very conservative figure — $10 billion for the flight of foreign currency, money which was sent to the industrialized countries — mainly the United States. And, lastly, as a prudent, conservative figure, since this is difficult to determine exactly, $5 billion would have to be added due to the overvaluation of the dollar.

In order to understand these losses, let's take gold as an example. This was often used as currency — the most traditional currency — to measure the value of things. Imagine that you are lent a kilogram of gold at 6 percent interest. Historically, interest rates were not very high, and some countries — particularly some religions, such as Islam — denounce interest and even assert that charging interest constitutes robbery. But, let's leave aside these ethical and religious considerations and accept as normal the fact that someone who was granted a loan should repay it, plus some additional amount. Suppose you are lent a kilogram of gold and are asked to return a kilogram, plus 6 percent more gold, at the end of the year. Suddenly, however, the person who lent you the gold decides that you should give him a larger amount of gold, 35 percent more — which is more or less equal to the overvaluation of the dollar. You have received a kilogram of gold, while the lender is demanding that you return 1.35 kilograms of gold, plus 6 percent interest. If, in addition to this, that 6 percent interest is raised to 10 percent when it comes time to pay, the lender is demanding that you pay 1.35 kilograms of gold, plus 10 percent more. In short, you received a certain amount of gold, at a certain rate of interest, but are being pressured to return a larger amount, at higher interest — that is, you are being robbed in a way that isn't permitted by any religion.

How much does that amount to? Well, I'd have to have the exact figures on what part of the debt was in dollars, and how much interest was agreed upon in each case, to know exactly how much the loan and the interest on that dollar, overvalued by more than 30 percent, has cost the debtors each year.

It can be calculated that at least two-thirds of Latin America's debt was contracted with U.S. sources — that is, let's say $200 billion. Let's assume that that figure represents the actual debt in dollars — which is quite unlikely, since other credit sources also operate with dollars — and that the dollar is overvalued by 10 percent. You are increasing your real debt objectively by $20 billion, plus the corresponding interest.

If the dollar is overvalued by 30 percent, your objective, real debt in dollars has increased by $60 billion. The amount of dollars doesn't change, but each dollar is more expensive. Therefore, I have made a very conservative estimate that, in 1984, at least $5 billion was paid in interest on that increased value of the dollar.

To sum up, for the reasons I have mentioned, Latin America has transferred more than $70 billion in a single year in the form of money or merchandise for which it didn't receive anything in exchange.

Now, another analysis: How much of that transfer was illegitimate? Let's accept the normal interest on the debt. We won't call it illegitimate; we won't call it plunder. But normal interest — we won't adopt the Islamic concept. Instead, we'll adopt the Western, Christian one. For a given amount of money, a reasonable — though relatively high

— interest rate must be paid, for example 8 percent, which includes the devaluation, which isn't exactly the case of the dollar. So, then, what share of the $70 billion that is now being exacted from Latin America is illegitimate? For the deterioration in the terms of trade, $20 billion; for an interest spread of 12 percent instead of 8 percent — also a conservative assessment — $10 billion. It is estimated that, for each one point rise in the interest rate, the amount that Latin America has to pay increases by $3.5 billion a year. Then, add $10 billion for the flight of capital — that is, money that the country received for exports, for services rendered, even for loans, money that the country needs for investments and for development, which is sent abroad. And $5 billion for the overvaluation of the dollar.

Thus, in 1984, the Latin American economy has been arbitrarily, illegitimately deprived of $45 billion. A part of the world whose population doubles every twenty-five years and which faces terrible social, educational, housing, health, and employment problems is being illegitimately deprived of $45 billion — of $70 billion of expatriated resources, when the allegedly normal interest is added.

Those countries' economies cannot hold up under it; this is already the case. They are becoming aware of this problem and are reacting. A serious crisis is in the making. If the Western countries persist in maintaining this system of plunder, and no solution is found, I believe that there will be a generalized social explosion in Latin America. And, of course, I'm stating this fact and reiterating it precisely so that everyone will become aware of the problem. I've been asked, "What do you want, an explosion in Latin America?" And I've answered, "No, we want these problems to be solved; an explosion alone won't solve the difficulties."

We must struggle to solve this economic crisis, to solve the problem of the debt. And we must struggle for the New International Economic Order, which was adopted nearly unanimously by the United Nations ten years ago to promote international cooperation and protect the economies and development prospects of the weaker countries. It was proposed in order to put an end to — among other arbitrary actions in the economic relations between the developed and the developing countries — the problems I've just mentioned: the growing deterioration in the terms of trade and unjust, abusive financial practices, such as artificial interest spreads and the overvaluation of the richer countries' currencies. This is compounded by equally loathsome and selfish trade practices such as the dumping of highly subsidized products and the protectionist tariff and nontariff measures constantly applied by the European Economic Community, the United States, and the other industrialized nations.

I would like to cite a very current protectionist policy which is tied to the domestic subsidies that have affected many countries in Latin America and the Caribbean. In 1981, the U.S. imported 5 million tons of sugar, most of which came from Third World countries. In 1984, it imported only 2.7 million tons. That is, sugar imports have dropped — drastically — and are still dropping. It has been estimated that, for the coming period, the U.S. will import less than 1.7 million tons. This is because the United States is protecting and encouraging the production of beet sugar and corn syrup. The taxpayers must pay for those subsidies. The consumers must pay more for that sugar because its price isn't regulated by the law of supply and demand, so loudly championed by the capitalist system. Moreover, the market system, likewise so loudly championed, isn't respected. Thus, an artificial procedure of subsidies and prices is established.

What are the consequences for those countries that used to export that sugar to the United States? Their exports have been reduced by half, by two-thirds. In addition, there is a customs duty. What about the Dominican Republic, Jamaica, Colombia, Peru, Ecuador, and many other countries? I'm not speaking about Cuba — our quota was taken from us a long time ago, under the pretext of having to blockade our country economically so as to strangle the social changes, and was distributed among those countries. Now, it's being taken away from them. We don't know under what pretexts, because they haven't carried out any revolutions or moved away from capitalism. What will they do with their workers? What will they do with their plantations and with their industries? What will they do with their debts? What will they do with the interest to be paid on their enormous debts? Naturally, this aggravates the crisis.

The United States is doing the same with textiles: restrictions and quotas for textile imports from Latin America and steel from Brazil, Argentina, and Mexico. And so on and so forth. This is all against the principle of free competition, the principle of supply and demand, and its much-championed market principle. Other products of the emerging industry of the Latin American countries have even fewer possibilities.

The European position is even worse: it subsidizes sugar at very high prices and exports the surplus. It used to import millions of tons of sugar; now it is demanding a quota of 5 million tons on the world market. All of these measures drive sugar prices down, because, if the U.S. stops importing 5 million tons, if it cuts its import figure in half, and if Europe stops importing and becomes a larger exporter, the surplus sugar goes on the world market and prices fall. Then Japan buys cheaper sugar, Canada buys cheaper sugar, and many other rich industrialized countries buy cheaper sugar. Yet, other countries have an unlimited need for this and other foodstuffs, but don't have the necessary purchasing power.

Europe subsidizes meat. In the past, it used to import it; now, it is a meat exporter. The European Economic Community meat producers are paid $2,500 a ton, and the meat is then exported for $800 a ton. So, meat from Argentina, Uruguay, Colombia, Brazil, Costa Rica, Panama, and other Latin American countries confronts a depressed world market price of $1,150 a ton. Just as with sugar, many Third World countries need meat, but they don't have the necessary purchasing power. Their own exports are depressed. Their main client, the industrialized world, is paying increasingly laughable prices.

In order to produce sufficient food for a large population, you need technology, fertilizers, pesticides, machinery, and energy, and you have to get them from the industrialized world or from the great fuel exporters at increasingly inaccessible prices. Investments, a technical culture, and scientific expertise are also needed. None of this is within their reach. They can't produce them, and they can't buy them. This is the tragedy.

The New International Economic Order calls for an end to such trade practices — indeed, abusive and unjust; they can't be described as anything else — by the richer, more industrialized countries. How can the Latin American countries be expected to develop when, in addition to their being paid less for their exports and charged more for their imports, their hard currency is drained away through the mechanism of the flight of capital, their exports are restricted, they are subjected to devastating forms of unfair competition, the dollar is overvalued, and they are charged arbitrarily high interest rates on the enormous debts that have been imposed on their people?

All of this constitutes a system of privileged economic relations for the industrialized countries, which are not particularly enthusiastic about giving up those privileges. The Third World countries — which for centuries were colonies and suppliers of exotic products, raw materials, and cheap fuel — are not to blame for their economic backwardness.

The per capita product of the Latin American countries as a whole has decreased. The gap separating them from the industrialized countries is growing ever wider. It is a sustained and fatal trend that must be reversed.

Mervyn M. Dymally: How do you respond to the often

repeated charge that Latin America has a moral responsibility to repay its foreign debts?

Fidel Castro: Let me tell you what happened with that money. Traditionally, debtors used to go to the banks to borrow money. In recent years, that practice has been reversed. The banks amassed huge sums; among other things, they collected the financial surpluses of the oil-producing countries during the oil-price boom, and some industrialized countries had accumulated huge sums of money. The role of the banks is to raise money, lend money, and earn interest. The banks went out to look for new people to lend to, and they lent a lot of money.

Some twenty or twenty-five years ago, Latin America had practically no debt. Now, it amounts to $360 billion. What did that money go for? Part of it was spent on weapons. In Argentina, for example, tens of billions of dollars went for military expenditures. The same was true of Chile and other countries. Another part of that money was embezzled, stolen, and wound up in foreign banks, frequently in Switzerland and the U.S. Another part returned to the United States and Europe as a flight of capital. Whenever there was talk of devaluation, the more affluent people, out of mistrust, would change their money for dollars and deposit it in U.S. banks. Another part of that money was squandered. Another part was used by some countries to pay for the high price of fuel. And, finally, another part was spent on some economic programs. Let's grant that.

You say that these nations have a moral responsibility. When you talk about nations, you're talking about the people: the workers, the farmers, the students, the middle class — that is, the doctors, engineers, teachers, and other professionals — and other social sectors. What did the people get out of the $360 billion that was spent on weapons, deposited in U.S. banks, misspent, or embezzled? What did the people get out of the overvaluation of the dollar or the interest spread? They got absolutely nothing. And who has to pay for that debt? The people: the workers, the professionals, and the farmers. Everybody has to make do with reduced wages, reduced incomes, and make huge sacrifices.

Where is the morality of imposing measures that result in a bloodbath in an effort to make the people pay the debt, as was the case in the Dominican Republic, where the International Monetary Fund's measures resulted in dozens of people being killed and hundreds more shot? The people have to protest, because they are being forced to pay a debt that they didn't contract and that brought them practically no benefits.

That's why we say that the payment of the debt is an economic impossibility, a political impossibility. You would practically have to kill the people to force them to make the sacrifices required to pay that debt. Any democratic process that tries to impose those restrictions and sacrifices by force will be destroyed. Lastly, it's a moral impossibility, for the reasons I've already stated.

Therefore, I think that it's much more moral to cancel the debt, which would benefit billions of people — I'm talking not just about Latin America's debt, but about the debt of Africa and Asia, which affects the lives of over 70 percent of mankind. It is more moral to cancel that debt than it is to spend the money on weapons: chemical weapons, nuclear weapons, biological weapons, aircraft carriers, battleships, strategic missiles, and "star wars" weapons programs. What is truly immoral, an act of bad faith, and practically a betrayal of mankind, is to force the people to go hungry; to live in poverty; to live in the worst material, educational, cultural, and health conditions in order to spend a trillion dollars on weapons and military activities every year. This is what is now being spent on preparing the conditions for a catastrophe, to kill hundreds of millions of people, and perhaps to even wipe out mankind. To those who make such statements, we must say that that is what is really immoral — not the cancellation of the debt, whose payment cannot be exacted from people who received nothing, no benefits, from that money.

Jeffrey M. Elliot: How would you assess the net effect of the United States's economic boycott on Cuba? How long can Cuba survive without U.S. trade?

Fidel Castro: Well, if you make the mathematical calculations — which we have done — you can detail the consequences of the blockade. It has already cost us billions of dollars. In transportation alone, to cite just one example, if you have to bring your imports from Japan or Europe, if you have to bring the goods you could otherwise have purchased in the U.S. from a place that is ten or twenty times as far away, you have to spend several times as much on transportation. If, in addition, you have to go to other places to find the goods that you couldn't buy in the U.S., you may also have to pay a higher price, because the trader, the seller, knows that you have no alternative but to buy that merchandise in that country. If you calculate the damage done to Cuba by depriving her of her sugar quota and the price difference between what we would have received from the United States under the existing agreements and the prices at which we had to sell that sugar in Japan and other countries, it's a lot of money.

If you calculate the damage caused by cutting off all supplies of spare parts, specific materials, and equipment for industries based on U.S. technology, you can see that the damage was considerable.

Some things were even more painful, however, because they caused damage to human beings. When you can't buy medical equipment that is made exclusively in the United States or a given medicine that is needed to save a life, the consequences of the blockade cease to be just economic; they are of a human dimension. When someone in any country is the victim of a measure that may cost him his life, there are legal procedures for claiming material compensation. For example, an enormous, justified claim has been lodged in India for the deaths of thousands of people caused by a lethal gas leak at a pesticide plant owned by a U.S. transnational. But, leaving aside those aspects, the blockade has cost our country's economy billions of dollars; we estimate it to be about $10 billion. Still, we've held out, and we can go on holding out. We've held out for twenty-six years, and we can hold out for another twenty-six years. We can hold out for another hundred years without trading with the United States, because we were forced to make greater efforts, to be more austere, more efficient. In other words, from the damage caused by the blockade, we have developed certain virtues that are of enormous value for a developing country. We have struggled to find alternative solutions, and we have found them. We have excelled at our work and have turned the U.S. economic aggression into a motivating force.

We have developed economic relations with the other socialist countries and established a kind of new international economic order in our relations with them. We aren't victimized by the law of unequal trade relations, protectionism, interest spread, an overvalued ruble, protectionist measures, or dumping by the other socialist countries. As a result, we have established a solid foundation for our country's economic and social development, which is guaranteed. We already know what we are going to do during the next fifteen years in all fields of economic and social development — in the industrial, agricultural, housing, educational, cultural, sports, and medical programs.

Despite the blockade, there are some areas, such as public health and education, in which our achievements come very close to those of the United States, and we expect to surpass it in the not-too-distant future. That is, we use our resources rationally to achieve sustained economic development in the interests of the people. We certainly won't adopt any such measures as reducing old-age pensions, cutting off aid and medicines for the sick, or reducing hospital and school appropriations. We don't sacrifice social programs — as they do in the U.S. — for the sake of building aircraft carriers, MX missiles, and other engines of war that the world abhors.

You can see the difference. While the United States has imposed a policy of sacrificing social assistance and social expenditures, in our country these are top-priority items. Rather than freezing them, as has been suggested in the U.S., they are increased every year as our economic performance improves. This is why Cuba is the only Latin American or Caribbean country which hasn't suffered from this crisis. We haven't been exposed to the crisis, except as it affects the 15 percent of our trade that is carried out with Western countries — which, of course, charge high prices for their products, pay low prices for ours, and force us to pay high interest rates in convertible currency on our foreign debt, which is relatively modest. But 85 percent of our trade is within the socialist community, and this is what gives us a solid foundation for the sustained growth of our economy. And, during these years of crisis, when the Gross Domestic Product and per capita product of the Latin American countries as a whole dropped, Cuba's Gross Social Product — that is, its economy — grew by 24.8 percent and its per capita product grew by 22.6 percent in the 1981-84 period. This is recorded in the annual economic reports of the United Nations Economic Commission for Latin America and the Caribbean, in which Cuba's situation can be contrasted with that of the rest of the Latin American countries.

The growth of the Cuban economy during the 1981-84 period is higher — much higher — than that of the rest of the Latin American countries. In Argentina, the Gross Domestic Product decreased by 6 percent; in Bolivia, by 16.1 percent; in Brazil, by 0.3 percent; in Chile, by 5.4 percent; in Peru, by 3.8 percent; and in Uruguay, by 13.9 percent. The list is quite long. I'm not referring to the figures on health and education, where our country is in first place among all the Third World nations and ahead of several industrialized countries, as well. We have no problems of unemployment, begging, slums, prostitution, gambling, or drugs. Not even alcoholism.

This is why we are morally entitled to speak about the present economic crisis and Latin America's debt. We don't have to keep silent. This is precisely why we are denouncing it energetically. But we can feel secure because, fortunately, we depend very little on the Western world, and we don't depend at all on economic relations with the United States. I wonder how many other countries in the world can say the same.

Mervyn M. Dymally: Let's daydream a bit. What would happen if the United States were to resume its trade relations with the Cuba? What effect would it have on the Cuban economy?

Fidel Castro: I believe that the United States has fewer and fewer things to offer Cuba. We export sugar, but the U.S. is reducing its sugar imports, nearly eliminating the sugar quotas of many Latin American countries. What sugar are we going to sell to the United States? The U.S. is drastically restricting its imports of Latin American steel. We can export some steel for construction, but there's no market for it in the United States. The U.S. is imposing extremely low textile quotas on the Latin American textile-exporting countries to protect its own textile production. The textiles made in the new modern textile mills that our country has built and in the old ones, many of which have been modernized and expanded, could not be sold to the United States.

As regards tourism, the demand is now greater than our hotel capacity. Lifting the blockade would imply an advantage only in the long run. I'm not going to say that we wouldn't derive some benefit, because that wouldn't be true. There might be some practical advantages. Perhaps some goods that now have to be acquired in distant third countries could be obtained in the United States, with lower freight costs and speedier delivery. We might purchase certain medical equipment manufactured in the U.S., some recent pharmaceutical products — things of that sort. But it wouldn't be anything out of this world, because it would be inconceivable for us to start buying Cadillacs and other luxury items from the United States if our relations were normalized someday. We haven't the slightest intention of spending a single cent on luxury items. The U.S. can go on exporting those things to other Latin American countries, to millionaires and other people who have money to spend on such items, even though their countries derive no benefit from such purchases; actually, it's the opposite, more debts with more squandering.

But, frankly speaking — I like frankness — economic relations with the United States would not imply any basic benefit for Cuba, no essential benefit. If trade relations with the U.S. were renewed tomorrow, and if we were able to export our products to the United States, we would have to start making plans for new lines of production to be exported to the United States, because everything we are now producing and intend to produce in the next five years has already been sold on other markets. We would have to take them away from the other socialist countries in order to sell them to the U.S., and the socialist countries pay us much better prices and have much better relations with us than does the United States.

We export our citrus fruit, a large part of our sugar, a large part of our nickel, and other products to the other socialist countries, which not only pay us much higher prices and sell their products to us at lower prices, but also charge us much lower interest for credits and reschedule our debt for ten, fifteen, or twenty years without interest. In fact, what are we supposed to do? There's an old folk saying that goes, "Don't swap a cow for a goat!" [Grins]

Jeffrey M. Elliot: Has Latin America's inability to repay its foreign debts affected its ability to negotiate new loans?

Fidel Castro: They don't need new loans. They don't need them. If they're paying $40 billion now — and they'll have to pay $40 billion every year if the debt doesn't continue to grow — that will mean $400 billion in ten years, with enormous sacrifices. It will be very difficult to convince the people to do this. They don't need loans. They can lend themselves the $40 billion and the $400 billion for development programs. The people will understand the need for such sacrifices and for implementing austerity measures for their development. Now, they are asking the people to make sacrifices that will promote backwardness, decrease the per capita product, and reduce the Gross Domestic Product. But they can persuade people to make sacrifices for the sake of growth and development.

Banks can't offer them more resources than they can offer themselves. For example, if Brazil is paying $12 billion a year in interest on its debt, it doesn't need any loans. If it invested that $12 billion, it would have $120 billion for development purposes in ten years. Mexico, with great restrictions, is exporting $23.5 billion worth of products while importing only $10 billion worth. It could invest more than $10 billion a year instead of paying the interest on its debt. That makes over $100 billion in ten years. If Argentina is paying $5 billion, that would amount to $50 billion in ten years.

No one can lend those countries such enormous sums for development. If anyone did, in a few years, they would be paying $60 billion a year in interest instead of the almost $30 billion they are now paying. That is, sacrifices would continue; they would be even greater. The economy would grow just to pay the interest to the banks. The situation can be compared to that torment in Greek mythology in which a man is doomed to push a large stone uphill for all eternity, a stone that always rolls down again before reaching the top.

I've cited several examples. The same could apply to Venezuela, Colombia, Ecuador, Peru, Uruguay — almost all the other Latin American countries. Then no one would have to lend them money; they could deposit that money and use it for development. No one could take reprisals against those countries or blockade them economically. The industrialized world can't do without the underdeveloped countries' trade. They can't do without their raw materials; they can't do without their minerals; they can't do without their fuel; they can't do without their chocolate.

Can you imagine an industrialized society — Switzerland, England, France, Spain, Italy, the Federal Republic of Germany, the United States, or Canada — without chocolate? Can you imagine those countries without coffee, tea, or cashew nuts to go with their drinks? Can you imagine them without nutmeg, cloves, peanuts, sesame seeds, pineapples, and coconuts or coconut oil for their mild and fragrant soaps? Life would be very sad and unpleasant in the industrialized countries if the steel, copper, aluminum, chemical, and power industries were also to stop. They can't do without these things.

Therefore, the power of decision no longer rests with the rich nations. If you tell them, "Lend, aid, cooperate, and be fair," ten or fifty years could go by without their paying you any attention. With this crisis, in which the gigantic debt is nothing more than an expression of systematic and historical plunder, the decision is now in the hands of the Latin American and other Third World countries. With the money they are handing over, they are morally and rightfully entitled to decide to suspend payments. This action isn't new; it's as old as Roman law. Loans, moratoriums, payments, and defaults all existed 2,000 years ago — sometimes decreed by the state, at other times by the debtors themselves. Of course, in those times in Rome — which was as democratic as the United States and which had a Senate like its Senate and a Capitol like its Capitol — when someone couldn't pay his debts, he was hauled into court and declared a slave. Enslavement for indebtedness lasted for millennia, from the time of Greece and Rome. Even recently, there were countries where people who couldn't pay their debts were declared slaves. What good are human rights and all man's achievements during the last two millennia? The industrialized countries could never shackle and enslave 4 billion people in the world, nor have they needed to up until now, because what they have done is to exploit them as if they were slaves. Today, they work almost exclusively for the benefit of the industrialized countries. They are slaves without chains, and they could very well proclaim their freedom before the industrialized world.

That has been done many times. During the past century, the slaves in Haiti declared themselves free. The freedom of the slaves in the United States was also proclaimed. This has happened in many parts of the world. No one has ever questioned the justice of that. This debt may become the chisel with which the economically enslaved peoples of the Third World begin to break their chains.

The cancellation of the debt would simply be an absolutely moral, absolutely unobjectionable, proclamation of freedom. This is clear: they don't need loans of any kind. Moreover, the industrialized world would benefit, because the developing countries would have greater buying power. Instead of importing $10 billion worth of goods, for example, Mexico could import $20 billion worth; Argentina could import $8.5 billion worth instead of $4.2 billion worth. This would also be the case with Brazil and the rest of the Latin American countries. Where would they buy finished products, materials, and agricultural, transportation, and industrial equipment? From the United States, Europe, and Japan. The Third World's buying power would increase every year by $80 billion — which, if well invested, could guarantee the sustained growth of their economies if the economic principles proclaimed by the United Nations were applied. This would mean more exports for the industrialized countries, greater use of installed capacity, and more workers employed.

Unemployment is the main problem in the industrialized world. They would increase employment and industrial profits, the export companies would export more, investors abroad would make larger profits, and the banks would recover their money. I'm not suggesting that the banks go under. I'm not suggesting that the banks lose their money. I'm not suggesting that the taxpayers pay more taxes. I'm suggesting something very simple: to use a small percent of military expenditures — which wouldn't be more than 12 percent — so that the creditor states could assume the debts to their own banks. This way, neither the banks nor the depositors would lose; to the contrary, the banks would have that money guaranteed. Who could guarantee this better than the rich and powerful industrial states of which the Western nations are so proud? If they consider themselves capable of dreaming up and waging "star wars," while giving barely a thought to the risks involved in a thermonuclear conflict that would in the first minute destroy a hundred times more than what is due their banks — in short, if the idea of universal suicide doesn't scare them, why should they be afraid of something as simple as the cancellation of the Third World's debt? What is the only thing that would suffer? Military spending. I believe that this is absolutely moral — and, furthermore, reassuring and healthful. This way, the solution of the Third World's economic problems would be associated with peace, with international détente, which is what all countries are now demanding.

No demand could be fairer or more moral than to end the arms race, to reduce military spending. This, in essence, is what I'm suggesting. I'm not saying that the banks shouldn't be paid. I am suggesting that the creditor state take over the debt to its own banks. That is the essence. It's a simple accounting operation. It's not going to close a single factory. It's not going to stop a single ship along its route. It's not going to interfere with a single sales contract on the market. To the contrary, employment, trade, and industrial and agricultural output and products would be increased everywhere. It isn't going to hurt anyone. The only adverse effects would be on arms and military spending, neither of which provides food, clothing, education, health, or housing for anyone. That is the formula I am suggesting.

Frankly, it seems to me that this takes everybody's interests into account. That's what's good about the formula: it hurts no one and benefits all.

Mervyn M. Dymally: Suppose the United States were to cancel the debt and, in cooperation with Latin America, provide a massive foreign assistance program. Would this action significantly alter your view of the United States and result in an improvement in U.S.-Cuban relations?

Fidel Castro: Let me answer your question this way. What is needed is for the debt to be canceled, because that will benefit the United States, international trade, and all countries. This would be of great help in overcoming the crisis, because, as a matter of fact, not even the U.S. has come out of the crisis. To the contrary, the U.S. is creating its own conditions for a bigger crisis.

During the last four years, the Reagan administration used its monetaristic policy and the United States's economic power so skillfully that it imposed a financial policy, a monetary policy, on the rest of the world. It forced not only the Third World countries — who could do absolutely nothing — but also its Spanish, French, Italian, English, West German, and Japanese allies and everybody else to accept it. Through its Federal Reserve Bank, the United States decided how much money there should be on the market, what the interest rates should be, and what economic policies to impose on the world — exclusively to solve is own economic difficulties: inflation, unemployment, and economic stagnation.

Moreover, this was associated with an arms race without new taxes, like during the Vietnam War. Economists know that the expenditures of the Vietnam War were one of the causes of the high inflation that hit the world economy. The United States spent hundreds of billions of dollars without raising taxes, because the war was so unpopular that the people would have balked at paying for it through new taxes.

Now, the United States is spending more than it did on the Vietnam War — and it is promoting rearmament and the arms race without raising taxes. It has tried to pay for it partly by cutting back public spending: assistance to senior citizens, the sick, and the schools — all those measures that have been discussed so much in the U.S. But those savings aren't enough, because military spending has grown enormously: from $135 billion in 1980, to $277 billion in 1985, to $314 billion in the coming fiscal year. That's not money for developing industrial technology or for making industry more efficient and productive. All that money is spent on very expensive equipment that contributes absolutely nothing to the economy. That's a fact.

What did this administration manage to combine? An arms race without raising taxes, a reduction in inflation, an increase in production, and a decrease in unemployment, which is truly marvelous. It's as if it had an Aladdin's lamp or the wild ass's skin of which Balzac spoke in his novel. But you could ask the wild ass's skin for only three things, and Reagan has already asked it for much more. Generally, those magic things don't grant an unlimited number of requests. They set a limit: three things, four things, or five things. I've listed four things here: rearmament without raising taxes, the reduction of inflation, an increase in economic activity, and a decrease in unemployment. Someday, the members of the brain trust that gave Reagan this formula will have to be found and given citations and maybe decorated with an award that could be called the "Order of the Machiavellian Prince," because they are certainly very intelligent people who know the secrets of these mechanisms and came up with what Reagan needed: to come to the election with less inflation, more employment, more production, and, in addition, almost $300 billion in military spending without raising taxes. Now, there are more battleships, aircraft carriers, bombers, nuclear submarines, cruise missiles, and arms of all sorts. That is how Reagan ran for reelection. He got all that.

But it makes you wonder. Money doesn't fall from the sky like rain; it has to come from somewhere. It makes you wonder how Reagan accomplished all this and how it was paid for. I think that's a question the U.S. citizens must ask themselves — and what the consequences will be after that. Well, for example, there is one: the public debt, which took 205 years to reach $1 trillion, increased by $650 billion in just three years of the Reagan administration, 1981-84. By the end of 1986, after five years of the Reagan administration, it will amount to more than $2 trillion. I'm using U.S. trillion, which is equal to the English billion: a million million.

The economists advising Reagan have managed to achieve in five years what it took all other presidents of the United States 205 years to do. There's no doubt it's an Olympic record. In addition, the budget deficit has already come close to $200 billion, and, at its present rate, it should reach $222 billion during this fiscal year. That's another Olympic record.

It should be borne in mind that in February 1985, in just twenty-eight days, the deficit rose $20.5 billion. Last year's trade deficit was $123 billion. An Olympic record. Three Olympic records. This year, the trade deficit is estimated at $140 billion. In February 1985, the figure was $11.4 billion — the highest since September 1984, when it amounted to $11.5 billion.

I ask you: Where does this money come from? How can this "miracle," this United States "miracle," be explained? How has Reagan managed to turn water into wine? How did he work the miracle of multiplying the fish and the loaves? I believe that, on the basis of this experience and what we are witnessing, it may be necessary to found a new church, because we are witnessing "miracles." And, obviously, we believe in "miracles." There may still be other "miracles" to see. Where does the money come from? From everybody. There are other "miracles." One way or another, they have managed to collect this money from the Japanese, the Germans, the English, the Italians, the Spaniards, and all the other industrialized and Third World countries and have brought it to the United States. This is an unprecedented phenomenon.

Foreigners have invested close to $200 billion in U.S. bonds. That is growing. What we have to do now is estimate the total amount of foreign deposits in the U.S. — which, as the *Washington Post* recently stated, is living above its level of production, above its level of productivity, and is becoming the country with the largest debt in the world. It is certain, most certain, that the United States alone already owes more than all the Latin American countries put together. Reportedly, its debt is close to $600 billion. We would have to ask the U.S. economists, the experts — there are a lot of them, and they have computers — to gather the information so that we, "the academics," can know how much the United States owes.

Of course, I suspect that the U.S., which has received overvalued dollars during these years, will try to pay with devalued dollars in the future. It will surely have a different policy as a debtor than as a creditor. It lent cheap dollars and is collecting expensive ones; it obtained loans and deposits in expensive dollars and will try to pay with cheap ones.

I'd like to imagine what the consequences of all this will be on future inflation — what the consequences will be and the impact this will have on the purchasing power of the U.S. dollar, how much the inflation will amount to, and if the "wizards" advising Reagan know when this phenomenon is going to take place — for it will take place, unquestionably. What will be the consequences for the future U.S. economy of spending $2 trillion in only eight years for military purposes, instead of investing it in industry, technology, and economic development? The only significant development has been registered by the arms industry, but weapons aren't goods that the population can consume. Rifles, bullets, bombs, bombers, battleships, and aircraft carriers increase neither the wealth nor the productive capacity of a country. They can't meet any of man's material or spiritual needs. You can't even fish with those boats; you can't do anything with them that's useful for human life, health, or the struggle against cancer and other diseases that kill so many United States citizens every year.

There are three diseases that kill millions of U.S. citizens: cancer, heart disease, and circulatory problems. I don't have the exact figures, but, in a population of 240 million, you can estimate that over a million people die every year from these three causes. No war ever killed so many U.S. citizens. If some of that money could be invested in fighting these diseases — and everybody knows that not enough resources have been earmarked for this — the life of the people in the United States and in many other countries of the world would be prolonged.

That $2 trillion doesn't produce even an aspirin; it doesn't solve a single headache. Someday, people are going to be sorry that the U.S. economy's industrial facilities aren't much more efficient, more productive. They're going to be sorry that the environment has become more and more polluted. They're going to be sorry they haven't invested in hospitals, recreation facilities, schools, homes for the elderly, and housing.

Someone is sure to say, "Well, was disarmament the only option?" No, the alternative was to get rid of prejudice, lies, and anachronistic myths; to get rid of the far-fetched dreams of sweeping other ideologies and social systems off the face of the earth; to stop attributing the craziest, most absurd intentions to the adversary; and to talk with the Soviets and work sincerely for peace once and for all. After all, the Soviets understand these realities much better than the people of the United States. They were in closer contact with the tragedy of war. They have a greater concern and greater feeling of responsibility regarding the need for averting a nuclear conflict which would be catastrophic and — in all likelihood — suicidal for mankind.

A socialist can better understand — is better prepared to understand, from a theoretical point of view — the folly of spending on weapons the resources needed to meet the pressing problems of any human society. All socialist states know what can be done with those resources, both at home and abroad. A glance shows the poverty and disasters that plague our planet. The arms race is a crime against mankind. Why not opt for a serious, sincere effort to seek peace and cooperation among all countries, based on full respect for the sovereignty and the social system that each people has chosen for itself?

The consequences that these enormous arms expenditures will have on the economy of the United States are yet to be seen. They will have an impact on inflation, the country's development prospects, the people's welfare, the country's prestige, and its relations with the rest of the world. No matter how rich a country may be, it can't squander its wealth and that of others with impunity. I think it's high time for the people of the U.S. to reflect on this.

We know what happened in November 1984 under the bewitching influence of the "miracles." The impact in November 1988 is still to be seen. Some symptoms can already be observed. The Senate Finance Committee adopted a resolution calling for drastic measures against Japan — it was almost a declaration of a trade war against Japan.

It is public knowledge that the United States's 1984 trade

deficit with Japan was $37 billion, and that it is expected to reach $50 billion in 1985. The Japanese aren't producing battleships, MX missiles, B-1 bombers, or Trident submarines. They're investing in industries, in development, as they've done during the last thirty years, and that is why they have modern, automated machine, electronic, chemical, and steel industries. Moreover, they're more austere, better organized, and more disciplined than the people of the U.S., and it's only logical that they compete successfully with U.S. cars on that country's own domestic market. The United States will have to set quotas and adopt other measures against the free market and free competition. It will have to demand an equal share of the Japanese market and do a series of things that contradict what it preaches and claims as its economic philosophy.

I believe that there will be people in the United States — thousands of people educated in economic matters — who will worry about the consequences of this tremendous arms race without raising taxes. This, I feel, should be debated in the House, in the Senate, and by the academic community, to see if what will come after these "miracles" can be explained.

What is clear is that the economy has declined, not grown, in Latin America. Nor has it grown in most of the Third World countries. In Europe, it grew very little, while unemployment grew a lot. The United States did manage to reduce unemployment — from nearly 11 percent to approximately 7.5 percent. But in England, the number of unemployed rose to 3 million; in France, to 3 million; in Spain, to 2.8 million; and, in the Federal Republic of Germany, to a postwar record of 2.6 million. And unemployment is still growing. These things begin to explain the "miracles." According to official U.S. statistics, in the last quarter of 1984, purchases by the United States government amounted to more than $72 billion, a record figure. And the present administration and its economic advisers have produced "miracles" and broken all Olympic records in the fields of budget deficits, trade deficits, foreign indebtedness, and the growth of the U.S. public debt.

I ask you: What will be the consequences of this policy? I believe that the people of the U.S. have the right to ask this question — the representatives, the senators. And we, too, have the right to ask this question, because the Third World countries are also affected by those consequences, in one way or another. What is it all for? To improve people's lives, well-being, health, or security? No. If the United States had really become indebted and incurred all these deficits in order to develop its economy, to increase production, this could have been accepted, even though its doing so at the expense of the world wouldn't have been very honest. If that money had been invested to raise the standard of living, you could say, "That isn't correct, because the country shouldn't be mortgaged just for that." We couldn't do that in our country. But, if you became indebted for either of the first two purposes, at least you would feel that you'd created something. If you do nothing of the sort, if you don't build a single industry with that money — a factory, a school, or a hospital — and if you don't improve the environment or housing, in the end you have mortgaged the nation and created nothing. You haven't improved anyone's standard of living, and you've spent a fabulous amount of money on war material that will become totally obsolete and only good for scrap in ten or fifteen years.

That's my view of what's happening in the United States.

You asked me what my reaction would be if the United States canceled the debt and also offered massive assistance to Latin America. As I said at the beginning, the cancellation of the debt would suffice. This may happen if the U.S. becomes convinced that there is no alternative, or if the Latin American countries decide to unilaterally declare the debt canceled, which would be more likely. They may do this by common consent. If a policy of austerity was followed, those resources could be enough for development. No additional massive injection of funds would be needed in many of those countries. It would be more important to solve other problems: to obtain equitable prices — that is, to put an end to the growing deterioration of trade that favors the industrialized countries, to put an end to protectionist measures, and to end the practice of dumping. All of these issues become the most important thing. If the Latin American countries had received in 1984 what they received in 1980 from their exports, they could have earned an additional $20 billion solely on that account. That's just an example.

Naturally, the Latin American countries will have to adopt effective measures to avoid the flight of foreign currency that has also meant serious losses in the past. But, as long as the present monetaristic policy is in effect, as long as the dollar is overvalued, and as long as 12 to 13 percent interest is being paid, Latin Americans will try to send their money to the United States. If all these tricks are ended, and if Latin America stops sending $70 billion to the industrialized world every year, including the interest on its huge debt, no massive injections of money would be needed for development. Then, if you add the cancellation of the debt at the expense of a small percent of military expenditures, and the banks recover their funds, additional development loans could very well be obtained and repaid. If the United States were to spontaneously do what you say — if such an inherently selfish, neocolonialist system were capable of that generosity — a real miracle would have taken place, and I would have to start meditating on that phenomenon. I might even have to consult some theologians and revise some of my opinions in that field. If that were to happen, I might even enter a monastery. [*Laughter*]

Mervyn M. Dymally: Some argue that the conditions the International Monetary Fund places on the Third

World countries constitute a blueprint for economic and political disaster. Do you believe that IMF policies spell doom for the underdeveloped nations?

Fidel Castro: They undoubtedly presage an economic disaster, a political disaster, and a social disaster. They will engender an unprecedented crisis with unpredictable consequences. I know what many people in Latin America are thinking and what their state of mind is. This includes people from all social strata, with the most diverse ideologies. Furthermore, almost unanimous awareness is developing concerning the debt and the impossibility of repaying it, as well as on the question of the unjust, intolerable economic relations that have been imposed on the Third World. One way or another, this situation will have to change. The International Monetary Fund, which is causing a lot of harm, will ultimately deserve our gratitude, because it is creating a big crisis, and solutions will stem from this crisis.

It is a law of history that big problems have never been solved unless they reach crisis proportions. Mankind has never had sufficient foresight to act otherwise. So, then, the IMF and the system — of which the IMF is a tool — will trigger rebellion in the Third World countries, and the rebellion will promote the solution of these problems. This will involve not only the debt but also the unjust and already intolerable economic relations between a handful of rich, industrialized nations and over 100 nations in which three-quarters of the world's population live. This won't be solved by a miracle, proclamations, ideas, arguments, or someone's persuasion or subversion. No, the crisis is what will lead to a solution.

As you know, the United States did not become independent until there was a crisis. Slavery was not abolished in the U.S. until a crisis occurred. In more recent times, Roosevelt's New Deal — which, by the way, saved capitalism — was a response to the great crisis of the 1930s. We should recall that, on the eve of the catastrophe, the

U.S. economy seemed healthier and more prosperous than ever before. On the eve of the 1914 war, the economic and social catastrophe in the old empire of the tsars gave rise to the first socialist revolution. The independence of India, the revolution in China, the socialist community in Europe, and the end of the colonial system came out of World War II.

If you analyze major historic events and the important changes that have been wrought everywhere, you will see that such was always the case. What will come from the economic, social, and even ecological catastrophe from which the peoples of the Third World are suffering? Won't the huge foreign debt trigger great changes in international economic relations? In Latin America — I have no doubts about this — either these problems will be solved or great social upheavals will take place that will lead to wide-spread revolutionary changes.

Ultimately, as a token of gratitude, we might put up a monument to the International Monetary Fund, and we might even put up one to Reagan, too. All these things — all these policies — are helping to unite governments, to unite Third World countries, regardless of ideology, in de-manding and bringing about a change in the established economic relations. I have no doubt about this. I am con-vinced of it. I am certain. The International Monetary Fund has run out of arguments with which to refute the facts, the data, the figures, the realities. All their theses and tra-ditional formulas — all their prescriptions — are in crisis.

The representatives and theoreticians of this venerable institution can call together all the Latin American leaders, academics, professionals, economists, and left- and right-wing politicians in a big theater and present their formulas, defend their theses, and explain how the problems we're talking about should be solved. And maybe those men — who, twenty-five or thirty years ago, would have wel-comed them with brass bands and applause — will give them cold, ironic smiles. Now, nobody in the world be-

lieves what they say. The Brandt Commission was probably the last effort to introduce some reforms and put a bit of
flesh, life, and common sense on the old skeleton of the
system created in Bretton Woods at the end of World War
II for dominating and exploiting the natural and human resources of Third World countries. But no one paid it any attention.

Well, then, it's not merely a matter of an awakening.
You become aware of the problem when the problem exists
in its full dimensions and its full seriousness. Until then,
everything is theoretical speculation — the noble work of
visionaries. Now, the problem exists in its full dimensions.
I would say that this system of economic relations has fallen into its own trap and that the enlightened economic advisers — the brilliant "wizards" who worked those fabulous "miracles" we've already talked about — are creating
the basis for a major tragedy for the U.S. economy.

I'd like to say just one more thing. This morning, the
wire services carried a rather unusual piece of news: President Reagan was the first to arrive — very early — at the
New York Stock Exchange. Of course, that's because there
were reports that the U.S. economy's growth during this
first quarter was much less than it had been last year, and
that the dollar was beginning to lose ground on the international market. President Reagan appeared at the Stock
Exchange to boost the dollar, to inspire confidence in the
economy, because, since all of this was "magical," there
was a real need to conjure up the spirits. In other words, if
that much money doesn't come out of labor, production,
productivity, and the gold mines, it has to come from the
spirits. [*Laughter*] He had to go there to perform something
like a religious rite, to protect the U.S. economy against
misfortune and difficulties. But Reagan's early morning
visit to the New York Stock Exchange, in spite of his heavy
work load in Washington — the many visits of illustrious
guests with whom he is meeting — is truly symptomatic.
Maybe Hoover's ghost was haunting the Stock Exchange,

and the evil spirits had to be exorcised.

Jeffrey M. Elliot: How likely is it that the present economic crisis will, in fact, serve to unify Latin America and produce a single, regional approach to solving these problems?

Fidel Castro: I think it will. I feel that one of the consequences of this unprecedented crisis and of this debt will be that it will unify the criteria of the Latin American political leaders in the search for joint action. This will happen because they are all aware of the vital need to find a solution for these problems. It's a matter of survival for the Latin American countries and, of course, of the survival of the current processes of democratic openings, as well as a matter of survival for them as the leaders of these countries. If you're dying of thirst in the desert, you need water. If you're at sea and your ship sinks, you need a raft. If you're going to be hanged, about to die, you need at least a knife to cut the rope. And that is the situation of the Latin American countries and of their political leaders. This struggle to find a solution is supported by the entire world: left, center, and right; beggars and millionaires; landless peasants and big landowners. It's a problem that affects everyone, and those who have the most possessions know the consequences of social upheaval. Yes, I believe that this will be an element that will undoubtedly promote unity of action.

Mervyn M. Dymally: Let's go to your neighbors in the Caribbean. Increasingly, these island states are becoming dependent on the United States for economic assistance, in order to meet the present crisis. Could these nations be significantly helped by increased grants and loans from the United States?

Fidel Castro: In today's world, the mere fact that a country is small, in both territory and population, constitutes a problem for development, because most of the technologies are based on a scale of production for a much wider market. Those scales tend to increase.

Everyone knows, for example, that proportionally a 2,000-kilowatt power plant consumes more fuel per unit of electric power produced than a 300,000-kilowatt thermoelectric power plant. Everyone knows that a nuclear power plant is built with reactors of at least 400 megawatts. Smaller reactors aren't even built.

In some international forums, Cuba has expressed the need to find a technical solution for this problem, which makes it impossible for many small oil-importing countries to use nuclear power. Nor can these countries receive electric power from another country, because they are geographically isolated.

Take the case of Europe and the Soviet Union. They have big power transmission lines, which transfer electric power from east to west and vice versa every day from the big plants located all over the country, so that each area receives what it needs during the hours of peak demand. When it is 8:00 at night in an eastern city, it could be 4:00 in the afternoon in a western city. This allows the power plants to operate at full capacity. They even transfer electricity to some of the European socialist countries — and, I believe, in some cases, to Western European countries. I suppose the United States does the same with its power plants, and the same is true for the gas and oil pipelines, roads, and railways that link the socialist and other European countries. Nothing like this could take place among the small nations of the Caribbean.

When a country is an island — even when the island isn't very small, as in Cuba's case — it can't receive gas, oil, electricity, or solid or liquid cargoes of any kind through any of the means used in continental territories. Everything must either be produced in the country or be brought in by ship. If the island is very small, its problems are multiplied. If you're going to set up a textile plant, the minimum capacity required for a rational, cost-effective scale of production is 25 million square meters of fabric. If you're dealing with a cement plant, you should set up a line that produces at least 300,000 tons a year. Smaller ones aren't even made. If you analyze a series of industrial branches, the problems of economic development in the small Caribbean countries turn out to be much more complex, much more difficult, precisely because they are both small countries and islands.

If you take all the Caribbean countries, the entire eastern Caribbean, it stands to reason that they need serious, creative theoretical solutions if they are to overcome these limitations and be anything more than places to go for tourism, pleasure, and gambling, with nice coconut trees and exotic nooks to be enjoyed by privileged travelers from the industrialized world. It's unquestionable that they need very close economic integration. Jamaica is somewhat larger and has a population of over 2 million; it can attain some autonomous development. The same holds true for Trinidad and Tobago. But most of those islands can't do without an economic community.

Let me remind you of an example: Western Europe, composed of a group of rich, industrialized nations. Those countries couldn't survive if it were not for the European Economic Community and economic integration. How can a group of small islands, which were colonies up until only a short time ago, survive and develop without integration? They need economic integration; there's no doubt about it. Only on this basis can they achieve some degree of industrial development, which is efficient in the various branches, taking into account the natural and human resources available on each of them, the group's potential market, and their export possibilities to other areas. Moreover, almost all of them speak the same language and have the same cultural background. They need an economic community. This, of course, would be a prerequisite for the viability of their independence.

It's perfectly understandable — I couldn't feel otherwise

— that the industrialized countries, even the United States, should open their doors to the products of these countries. I support this fully, because that's what I've been postulating as a general principle. The developed nations should open the doors of their markets to the products and exports of the countries that need development. That is an aspect that the so-called Caribbean Basin Initiative contemplates, though for a limited period of time. The project includes this positive element, but the concept is permeated by the idea that the transnationals are to take over those countries. The development of those islands is conceived as a matter of private business. This aid is offered to U.S. investors. Rather than national development with local entrepreneurs, it is viewed as transnational development with foreign entrepreneurs and based on cheap labor — the workers' wages being the only thing that would remain in the country. In exchange for that, these countries would be granted tariff and tax exemptions of all sorts, and even the chewing gum and soft drinks would have to come from the United States. It's the same old story of the banana and sugarcane republics. We're already familiar with that kind of development. It won't integrate the Caribbean countries or unite them. Rather, it will splinter them, make them compete with one another, and facilitate their manipulation. We can't agree with that concept at all.

In Puerto Rico — which once was presented as a model of this type of development — after over $20 billion was invested, largely in all sorts of polluting industries, there is a very large number of unemployed people, and almost half of the population receives food stamps in order to subsist.

Those eastern Caribbean islands — and many other regions of the world, as well — need large-scale international cooperation for their development. They can't even survive on their own resources. What is required is the kind of economic and social development that promotes the people's welfare — not the profits and business interests of

the transnationals, which would ultimately b
the market facilities offered to them.

In short, they need integration and internatio
ation; their development can't be carried out solely on the
basis of their own resources. It should be carried out not as
a transnational business, but to promote their people's
welfare and consolidate their independence and national
identity. Foreign cooperation is, therefore, essential. I believe that there are very few Third World countries — particularly these and other small islands and countries in
black Africa — that don't need considerable international
cooperation for their development.

Jeffrey M. Elliot: Let's assume the worst possible
scenario — namely, that the debt crisis continues to de-
teriorate. What impact will a major deterioration have on
democratic political institutions within Latin America?

Fidel Castro: It would mean a crisis, no matter what they
do. If there's a government like Pinochet's, it would imply
the crisis of Pinochet's government. If there's a government like the one that's just been elected in Uruguay and
there's no solution for this problem, it would mean a crisis
for the democratic opening in that country. In Brazil and
Argentina — it would mean a crisis for the administration
in any of those countries. It isn't a selective virus — not at
all. It affects everyone: dictators, democrats, right-wing-
ers, those in the center, left-wingers, everyone. Of course,
I wouldn't complain if this led to the rapid disappearance
of Pinochet's regime. What really hurts is that it could also
mean the rapid ruin, the rapid erosion, of all the governments that have emerged as a result of the democratic
opening and, thus, the crisis of all those processes, if they
aren't able to unite the forces inside and outside the country to wage and win the battle of the foreign debt.

In this case, I don't believe there will be new right-wing
military coups. Rather, there will be social upheavals that
will assume revolutionary characteristics with the possible

participation of progressive, nationalist sectors of the military. I maintain that the armed forces are in open retreat from government, precisely because of the crisis. Those countries have become unmanageable, and the military have left the government to the civilians. For the time being, they want nothing to do with the administration of the state, though this doesn't preclude the emergence of revolutionary movements within the military in some countries, as a result of the crisis. Whether it will be the civilians or the military or a combination of the two that assumes the responsibility, someone will have to tackle this problem. Under these circumstances, anything can happen.

Mervyn M. Dymally: Are you concerned that the industrialized world could or would attempt to blockade the Third World if the affected Latin American nations failed to repay their debts?

Fidel Castro: Nothing the industrialized world does could be worse than what's happening right now. Moreover, it's a political impossibility in today's world. One or two countries can be blockaded; 100 countries can't. The entire Third World can't be blockaded, for that would mean that the industrialized world would be blockading itself. What a few countries do will surely — with very few exceptions — be supported by the rest.

Jeffrey M. Elliot: What do you see as the major stumbling blocks to the successful resolution of the debt problem? Do you believe that your proposal will elicit widespread support among the Third World countries?

Fidel Castro: I believe that, up to now, the United States and the other industrialized countries have tried to postpone the problem and tackle it through separate discussions with each of the affected countries, making some concessions, such as the rescheduling of the debt, granting extensions for paying the capital, and coming up with formulas of that sort that don't solve anything, but only offer brief, spasmodic breathers that simply prolong the agony. The situation is being exacerbated economically and politically in all those countries, because any solution requires truly radical formulas — not just for tackling the debt, which is only a part of the problem. The debt is a consequence of the problem and its most visible symptom but not its cause. If the debt is canceled tomorrow, then a few years from now those countries will be either the same or worse off than they are now. In some cases, it wouldn't even solve anything now; their situation is so difficult that they wouldn't even get a breather if the debt were canceled.

I have shown you that there are some problems that are worse than the debt: depressed prices, the flight of capital, excessive interest, the overvaluation of the dollar, protectionism, and dumping. These deprive the Latin American countries of twice the resources they remit for what could be considered normal interest on loans. If the problem of the debt is solved and these problems remain, they will have gotten nothing but a breather.

Therefore, the industrialized countries have no rational, effective formula with which to face the crisis at present. None.

I believe that the main difficulty lies in a lack of understanding about the nature and seriousness of the problem. I'm not advocating social revolution in those countries. I'm not advocating the nationalization of foreign enterprises. I'm not advocating any of those steps. No. I'm propounding formulas in the financial sphere, which, I feel, would benefit all of the underdeveloped and even the developed countries. I've already spoken to you about this. The cancellation of the debt, in the way I've outlined, would be an important step toward emerging from the current international economic crisis. It would even help the foreign companies with investments in those countries, the companies that have trade relations with those countries, the companies that produce goods for those countries. And, in the creditor countries, the state wouldn't be hurt economically. To the contrary, they would raise their levels of employment and use of industrial capacity; their banks wouldn't suffer any losses; and their taxpayers wouldn't have to pay any more taxes.

If this is understood, if there is an awareness of this, I believe that the path toward a solution would be made much easier by means of dialogue, through agreements between the industrialized and the Third World countries. And, as I said earlier, the only thing that would suffer would be the irrational arms race, the frantic madness of weapons and war — and that, unfortunately, to only a very small extent. This would be a healthy measure, since we would begin to overcome the most shameful and dangerous disease of our times. If the New International Economic Order, which has been proclaimed and agreed upon by the United Nations, is implemented as an indispensable complement to the cancellation of the debt, that would really imply a greater reduction of military expenditures.

I've spoken with dozens of people, even many Latin Americans lately. And I haven't met one of any ideology, of any political or apolitical belief, who wasn't absolutely convinced that this was correct.

If we don't succeed in this, what will happen? Instead of there being a negotiated agreement between the parties, the Third World countries will impose this agreement. Let there be no doubt about it.

Essentially, the situation is as follows: it is materially impossible to pay the debt and its interest; therefore, due to this very elementary and understandable reason, the debt cannot be paid. It would take rivers of blood to force the peoples to make the sacrifices this would imply — for which they would receive nothing. No government would be strong enough to do this. This is worth analyzing, discussing, and solving in common agreement between creditors and debtors. We should never forget, even for an instant, that the initiative has passed to the nations that are being pressured to make this monstrous sacrifice.

If the debtor countries of the Third World are forced to decree a suspension of payments unilaterally, the industrialized countries will be left without any possible alternative for action. An economic blockade, an invasion of the Third World, a new repartitioning of the world as in past centuries, in order to guarantee raw materials and markets or to collect the debt, is simply impossible. Any rational person can understand this. They couldn't impose an economic blockade on any country or group of countries that declared a suspension of payments, because this would immediately lead to expressions of solidarity by all the other countries.

We are one big family, and times have changed a lot. Some madnesses have already been left behind, and others — such as several of the ones analyzed in the course of this interview — are on the way out.

I remember that, when I was in the fourth or fifth grade, when I began to study world geography — before I had any clear ideas about geography — I must surely have thought the world was flat, as had been believed during the Middle Ages, before Columbus came along. Someone must have taught me about these great discoveries before then, but, when I began studying world geography, I discovered many marvelous things: that the earth was really round; that there was a sun around which it orbited; and that there were other planets and millions of stars and even a moon, which orbited around our planet. Truly fabulous things.

Later, I learned about the great rivers, oceans, seas, gulfs, lakes, mountains, and other wonders of the world. All this was perfectly clear and understandable. I also began studying the political geography of the times. The maps of each continent were beautifully colored. All the English colonies in Africa, the Middle East, Asia, and

Oceania — including India, Burma, New Zealand, and Australia, of course — were in red. I remember this perfectly, and it had nothing to do with communism. That map was almost all red, and now that map — Canada was also red — would look like a communist world.

The color for the French colonies was the next most extensive one. I think it was yellow: in the Caribbean, Africa, Asia, the Indian Ocean, and the Pacific Ocean. Countries that are well known today, such as Algeria, Vietnam, and Syria, were mere anonymous spots of yellow on those maps. Some of those yellow spots, sometimes lost in the blue immensity of the oceans, are still a headache for France today.

Several days ago, [French President François] Mitterrand had to drop everything and travel thousands of miles to see if a solution could be found for the problems of the small island of New Caledonia and its severe political repercussions in France itself. Such a small island! Who would have said that when I was in the fifth grade? A large part of the map of Africa was in yellow, and it had nothing to do with China.

There were many other colors: orange, brown, green, gray, etc. When you looked at the map of Europe, you saw countries as small as Portugal, Belgium, Holland, and Denmark with large sections of the world's map, in which they could fit many times. Mozambique covered a considerable portion of the map, painted in the color which indicated the Portuguese colonies: Angola, another considerable section; the same color filled a section of Western Africa and was present in the tiny islands of Cape Verde, São Tomé and Príncipe, and even in India and Oceania. That small European country, where many people didn't even know how to read and write, owned large territories.

Then came the Dutch, with big territories in the East Indies. Belgium had the vast Congo; Denmark, the enormous space of Greenland, covered with ice and almost uninhabited, even if it were only a matter of prestige. Even Spain, as if in consolation for its decline from the times when the sun never set on its immense dominions, still had some territories in Equatorial Guinea and Western Sahara, whose people are our Spanish-speaking brothers in Africa. Those countries had carved up the world among themselves and were owners both of the land and of the natives. Even Mussolini waxed enthusiastic over his dreams of reestablishing the old Roman Empire. Libya, Somalia, and part of Ethiopia weren't enough for him. He invaded the only independent territory that was left in Africa, the remains of the ancient Kingdom of Ethiopia. A large part of China and all of Korea bore the colors of the empire of the Rising Sun. We students were taught this as if it were another natural phenomenon in the world, as natural as the mountains and the rivers. I never heard my teachers or professors make even the slightest critical analysis of those maps, and I was supposedly receiving a good education, so I could know and understand the world.

Years later, I was able to understand that all of this was an absurd madness, a great injustice, and a terrible crime, that that irrational yearning for colonial possessions was the cause of many wars over the centuries and that it was directly responsible for systematic, continual repartitions. However, nothing seemed more natural, moral, and fair to the civilized and Christian West, the world of the great thinkers and philosophers. The liberty, equality, and fraternity which one day shook feudal society was only for Europeans and whites. It was very difficult for that world to believe that the Indians, blacks, and Asians had souls. Socialism was still a distant idea: nothing disturbed that idyllic world of nascent, voracious capitalism.

On the map, Latin America was depicted as a group of independent countries. Later, I was able to see what kind of independence the Latin American countries really had, what kind Cuba, Central America, and the others had.

The colonized countries had no idea how weak the colonial powers were and what enormous, invincible, potential power lay in their patriotism and national dignity. Feats as revealing as the ones wrought by the people of Vietnam and Algeria hadn't yet taken place, though it's only fair to note that, by the end of the past century, Cuba had already shown that a small country could stand up to one of the mightiest European military powers.

How much has the population of the Third World grown in the last eight decades? How much has our political know-how, our sense of national dignity, and our awareness of our enormous potential power multiplied?

I wonder if the creditors really want to apportion these countries among themselves again; if they would really dare to try a show of force against the Third World; if they can even consider imposing an economic blockade against any country that may be obliged to declare a suspension of payments on the debt. In any such attempt, the industrialized capitalist world would find itself alone and isolated, reduced to a small group of countries from which some would be absent, as in the case of the group that rejects the Convention on the Law of Sea, the group that wants to disband UNESCO, or the group that supports South Africa's apartheid. So, in point of fact, there isn't the slightest possibility that they could impose an economic blockade on, intervene in, or redistribute these countries among themselves and return to the times when I was a fifth-grade student in elementary school, which really wasn't so long ago. [*Grins*] Nevertheless, many things have happened in the world since then.

Mervyn M. Dymally: If you could establish a new world economic order, upon what principles would it be based? What would be its chief elements?

Fidel Castro: Look, I think it's impossible for anyone, on his own, to define or to even outline all the aspects of what should constitute the New International Economic Order, in which new situations are constantly cropping up. These problems have been discussed at length in the United Nations; the corresponding documents have been accepted and adopted. At the initiative of Algeria, Mexico, and other countries, it was virtually unanimously defined and adopted in that organization, where all of the nations of the world are represented, more than a decade ago. It simply hasn't been implemented. The industrialized Western countries haven't even wanted to have the issue raised again — irrefutable proof of the hypocrisy and scorn with which they treat us. We must demand its implementation. This, precisely, is the problem. I am a convinced and determined defender of these ideas, in which many of the finest minds of the Third World invested thousands of working hours.

I believe that certain principles are fundamental: the starting point must be the fact that there is an immensely rich, economically, industrially, technologically, and scientifically developed world and that, on the same planet, near it, there is another world that is just the opposite, where 70 percent of the world's population now lives and where, by the end of the century — fifteen years from now — 80 percent will live, because the population of those countries is growing by 2 to 3 percent a year.

The countries that make up the Third World were colonies of the European powers in the not-too-distant past. The people of the United States recall that their country was once an English colony. The present industrialized countries — the former colonial powers and their more privileged colonies, such as the United States, where the African slave trade and slavery continued for almost a century after its independence — now constitute the main nuclei of industrial development in the Western world. They are historically responsible for underdevelopment because, for centuries, they benefited from plundering those countries.

Let me tell you something: it was the gold and silver that were extracted from the mines of Latin America that really financed much of Europe's development. That is a fact recognized by historians and economists. The present financial system didn't exist at that time; the gold and silver came from here. The resources contributed by the colonies — which also encompassed Africa and Asia — financed a large part of the economic development of Europe and the world capitalist system. The former colonial powers have a responsibility for underdevelopment and, therefore, a duty and a moral obligation to the peoples whose wealth they siphoned off for centuries.

I don't think that it's only the former colonial powers that have this obligation. I believe that all of the countries that, in one way or another, have achieved the privilege of development have the elementary duty of expressing solidarity with this immense area of poverty and underdevelopment. This is a human and moral principle. While once it was fraternity among men that was proclaimed and inscribed in the great slogans of the French revolution — and even the American revolution — now it is fraternity and solidarity among peoples that has to be considered. In fact, I believe that this principle should be an essential part of the concept of the New International Economic Order. It isn't just a matter of redress for a historic injustice, for which we may or may not be responsible. Rather, it is a moral imperative vis-à-vis the human race — even if we aren't to blame for the present tragedy. If these principles are taken as the starting point — principles that involve the ideas of justice and solidarity among peoples as they exist to a greater or lesser extent within each nation — then international cooperation should be one of the basic principles of that new order.

Aside from that, there are injustices, inequalities, inconsistencies, and selfish attitudes that must cease. If the industrialized capitalist countries really can't come up with a solution for their difficulties — sometimes because of the system's intrinsic irrationality, anarchy, and contradictions, since technology, resources, expertise, productive capacity, and culture aren't factors that limit satisfying their material and social needs — then I can find no justification for the protectionist policies that stunt the economies of the Third World countries, where billions of people live in subhuman conditions. If there is unemployment in the developed countries, it is entirely due to pure irrationality, because if full employment existed — that is, if all human resources available were used — working men and women could have a shorter workweek. Rest is also one of mankind's most prized possessions.

Dumping is an even more reprehensible practice, because it constitutes unfair competition based on financial and technological superiority over countries with weaker economies that are desperately in need of means of subsistence.

Unequal terms of trade, the deadly process through which the commodities of the vast majority of the Third World countries bring ever lower prices while the products they import from the industrialized countries become ever more expensive — a continual, worsening historic trend — is one of the most diabolical expressions of the present system of economic relations imposed on the world. You can't call it anything but the systematic robbery of our peoples' resources and the fruits of their labor.

The Third World countries produce products — coffee, cacao, precious wood, tea, spices, aluminum, copper, iron, manganese, chrome, medicinal plants, peanuts, sesame seeds, cashew nuts, coconuts, kenaf, sisal, or rubber — that the industrialized countries can't produce at all or can only produce in limited quantities. Those Third World products are frequently obtained without any mechanization, with very low productivity, grain by grain, leaf by leaf, in twelve- or fourteen-hour workdays, with the labor of men, women, children, adolescents, and old people.

For example, sugarcane is, with few exceptions, cut and loaded by hand and transported by ox cart. In general, all of the work is done in temperatures of thirty degrees centigrade or more, in humid climates, with seasonal work and starvation wages that don't amount to more than $60 or $80 a month. Generally, there is no medical care. Large families live in thatched-roof huts with dirt floors, going barefooted most of the time and poorly dressed all the time, with no unemployment compensation and beggarly pensions. Life expectancy is frequently less than forty years. There is premature aging, no education, no recreation, no comfort, no hope. Yet, in order to keep producing and just stay alive, those countries have to import high-technology, industrially processed products — even in the case of medical equipment and medicine — that involve high company profits and salaries of $1,000 and even $1,500 a month. With the prices they charge us, we pay for the companies' profits, high salaries, taxes, unemployment compensation, old-age pensions, social benefits, and advertising — even part of their military expenditures.

We often have to pay ten, fifteen, or twenty times as much for our own raw materials that have been processed as we were paid for them. What do we get for our products? Very low wages, no social security or unemployment compensation, no medical care, no education, no culture, no recreation, no hope of progress, premature aging, and early death. And things are getting steadily worse: the same amount of coffee, sugar, tea, copper, iron, and bauxite with which we used to buy a piece of medical equipment, some medicine, an irrigation pump, a bulldozer, a crane, a truck, a tractor, or a simple work tool thirty-five years ago now buys only a third as much. Every day there is more work. Every day there are more sacrifices. Every day there is more hunger for more people. Every day there is more poverty. The New International Economic Order, which was adopted by the United Nations, was designed to solve or at least mitigate these problems.

We have done this: we have obtained fair and stable prices for our exports, which are indexed to the prices of the products we import. We have obtained the new economic order in our relations with the rest of the socialist camp, and this, fortunately, has resulted in our industrial, agricultural, and especially social development. An average educational level of the ninth grade, a rate of only 15 children out of every 1,000 born alive who die before they are a year old, life expectancy of 73.5 years, and the fact that 85 percent of all Cuban homes have electricity are some of these results. These achievements could not have been realized without such terms of trade — not even with a fair social regime and an equitable distribution of social wealth.

I've presented some ideas about the New International Economic Order. Important concepts were also expressed regarding the transfer of technology, contributions of financial resources, and other aspects.

It's not so much a question of transferring resources to the Third World — many countries couldn't do without them, no matter what the circumstances. It's rather a matter of immediately ending the huge transfer of resources which, for instance, takes place every year from Latin America to the industrialized world, amounting, as I told you, to more than $70 billion, no less than $50 billion of which is in cash, under various headings: interest on the debt, the flight of capital, interest spread, and the overvaluation of the dollar. When the Charter of the Economic Rights and Duties of States was discussed in the United Nations ten years ago, this couldn't even be imagined in its full dimension. As an immediate measure, the cancellation of the foreign debt is indispensable. The United Nations already envisaged this at that time for the group of countries with greater difficulties. Now, very few countries — if any — don't have great difficulties. Today, they are divided into those with great difficulties and those with terrible difficulties. Therefore, there must be a general cancellation of the debt and its interest.

The industrialized world will lose nothing with the New

International Economic Order that was adopted by the United Nations.

At times, a European Economic Community country wants to solve the difficulties of a small farming sector of its population — which are not, in fact, problems related to hunger. It resorts to the often used recourse of subsidies, not only to supply the domestic market but also to export considerable amounts of products — such as sugar, meat, or other foodstuffs — that compete with many Third World countries' vital exports and that can also be produced in temperate climates, such as beet sugar or corn syrup.

It doesn't concern them at all that they are taking away markets and depressing the prices of basic exports from which hundreds of millions of people in the underdeveloped countries live. They don't even have a guilty conscience; they don't come up with other ideas. They aren't the least bothered about raising the cost of those products for their own domestic consumers or about violating all the principles of the free market and free domestic and international competition, which are the postulates of the philosophy for which they fought many bloody wars. Giving up the brutal neocolonialist practices applied to the Third World would not affect the industrialized countries at all; rather, it could promote a healthier, more stable, and more sustained development of the entire world economy.

For centuries, many believed that the end of colonialism would ruin Europe. On the contrary, history has proved that Europe never before developed so much or achieved higher living standards than when the colonial system collapsed. In Asia, too, the catastrophic collapse of the empire of the Rising Sun — which sought to guarantee raw materials, rubber, oil, and other resources by force — marked the era of Japan's greatest development, prosperity, and well-being.

When, instead of exploiting others, nations have been forced to live off their work and ingenuity, they have achieved wealth beyond expectations. Spain had one of the greatest colonial empires. All of Spanish America contributed fabulous sums of gold, silver, and other wealth to Spain for 300 years. Did Spain develop? All that money wound up in England, France, Holland, and other countries. In the era of industrialization, Spain remained the most underdeveloped country in Europe until the beginning of this century. Did the colonies help in the development of Spain? They helped in the development of Europe, but Spain did not develop. The industrial development of Spain began toward the end of the last century, when it was left without colonies and even lost Cuba, which was the last colonial gold cup.

Another example is a recent development that began in 1974. During the sudden spectacular rise in oil prices, which went from $2.50 to $30 a barrel, many felt that the economy of the industrialized countries could not withstand such price rises. Actually, the ones that didn't withstand them were precisely the non-oil-producing countries of the Third World, for which a new form of unequal exchange emerged. For example, twenty-four years ago, if they needed, say, one ton of sugar to buy four tons of oil, they now need two-and-one-half tons of sugar to purchase one ton of oil. The same thing happened with coffee, cacao, sisal, fibers, fruits, minerals — with everything the Third World countries produce. Tanzania, to name one concrete case, is a country that lives off many of these products and even exports meat produced from nomad herds. All of its exports are not sufficient to pay for its modest oil consumption, which is less than one million tons a year for a population of 18 million.

On the other hand, what happened with the industrialized countries? Nothing. They adapted. They developed programs to conserve the energy that they were squandering. They designed more efficient engines. They used coal once again. They developed nuclear programs, such as in France and other countries, and they started to exploit old wells, which had ceased to be profitable. As a result of those hikes in the price of energy, in eleven years, they spent over one trillion dollars while adapting to the new situation. Where did that money go? To United States and European banks. It returned to the industrialized capitalist countries. They handled it, lent it, increased exports to oil-exporting countries, made deals worth millions, and also sold unprecedented amounts of weapons. The shah of Iran multiplied his purchases of weapons from the United States. The United States sold Saudi Arabia and Iran tens of billions of dollars' worth of planes, radar equipment, and weapons of all sorts — which was really sad — and it made tremendous deals. How was the economy of the industrialized world harmed? The price of oil hurt the weak economies of the non-oil-producing Third World countries.

What economic impact could cancellation of the debt and the New International Economic Order have for the United States and the other industrialized countries? Actually, I think it would be much fairer and could significantly increase trade in agricultural equipment, medical equipment, machinery, and many other industrial and agricultural items. If the Third World countries get fairer prices for their basic exports, the Western industrialized countries would also benefit. This would generate employment and industrial development throughout the whole world. I believe all of that is possible. We only have to give up one thing: the madness of war and the ongoing, colossal arms race. This is obvious, simple, basic.

Now, then, if we want to be madmen, if we want to continue the arms race and keep this unfair economic order, we will continue along the path leading to large-scale famines, great social conflicts and — what is even worse and very probable — a large nuclear conflict, until all people, both sane and insane, are wiped off the face of the earth. By the way, it may also be said that not all madmen are in government, and not all who govern are mad.

Jeffrey M. Elliot: Do you discern sharp differences between the United States's approach to the economic problems in Western Europe and its approach to Latin America? If so, what?

Fidel Castro: Yes, unquestionably there are different approaches. The United States's relations with Western Europe and Japan are relations between industrialized and developed countries, involving some competition, some integration, and some cooperation — not unequal trade.

The following is proof of this: the transnationals have investments valued at $625 billion, only $150 billion of which is in the Third World. Of the $150 billion, 53 percent — that is, some $80 billion — is invested in Latin America and the Caribbean. This means that over 75 percent of the transnationals' investments are in the industrialized world. There are European companies in the United States and U.S. companies in Europe. The same holds true with regard to Japan and other industrialized countries. This phenomenon of unequal trade doesn't occur among them, even though the United States's economy prevails among the Western economies, and it is the one that sets the standards and makes the rules. There are difficulties, contradictions, among these nations that they are constantly discussing — between the United States and Japan, between the United States and Europe, between Europe and Japan. Even so, they get along just fine. They sometimes have so many resources, so much productivity, that they can permit themselves the luxury of working fewer hours and have a per capita income that is incomparably higher than that of the Third World. If the system were at all rational, still fewer hours could be worked and unemployment could be eliminated. But, naturally, the system itself demands a reserve army of the unemployed. There is a growing difference between the per capita income of the industrialized countries and the per capita income of the developing countries.

On the other hand, U.S. relations with Latin America are unequal and unfair, as are the relations between other industrialized countries and Third World countries. I've already gone into this at some length and explained how the Latin American countries transfer huge resources to the industrialized countries every year.

The main difference is that there are two types of relations: the ones existing among the industrialized countries themselves — relations of cooperation, integration, and trade on more or less equitable grounds — and their relations with Latin America, which are unfair and are based on ruthless exploitation. That is the essential difference.

Mervyn M. Dymally: During this interview, you have proposed a concrete solution to the debt crisis. How have the nations of Latin America responded to your suggestions? Do you expect them to embrace the plan?

Fidel Castro: I've been talking about this problem for quite some time now — for example, at the United Nations, in October 1979. In my speech, I called for the cancellation of the debts of the least developed countries and easier repayment terms for the other, more developed Third World countries. I also referred to the need for additional financial resources amounting to $300 billion for development assistance in the decade 1980-90, if the programs that the United Nations has proposed so often for that part of the world were to be implemented. Many of these problems — those of unequal trade, the protectionist measures, and other issues — were defined in 1979, when the great crisis of the 1980s had not yet occurred even though it was already in the offing. The present situation is very different.

I set forth those same problems in New Delhi in 1983, at the Summit Conference of the Movement of Nonaligned Countries, and in other international meetings, but — I repeat — there are two differences now: first, the crisis hadn't reached its most critical point, and, second, we were drawing up, arguing over, reasoning out, and requesting timely and appropriate measures. The United Nations's goals have not been met. The gap between the industrialized and the Third World countries is widening. Cooperation is needed. Resources are needed for development. I referred to all this at some length. That statement may have been very fair, but its importance was relative, because — and I repeat — the crisis hadn't reached its most acute point. We should analyze what has happened between 1979, when I raised this, and today. The facts about what has happened in each Latin American country are available.

Then, the decision was in the hands of the industrialized countries. They could afford to turn a deaf ear to the problem. The situation is now totally different; the crisis has become acute. The decision isn't in the hands of the industrialized countries; it is in the hands of the Latin American and Third World countries. The industrialized nations will now have to accept what these countries decide: whether they want to continue remitting fabulous sums of money for the debt service or not.

With respect to the Latin American countries' response, I can only tell you that these statements have awakened great interest in all nations and in all social sectors. What will the answer be? If I hadn't said a word about this — words now have a relative value, since the time has come for all to make great decisions — they would have to find a solution. They were going to reach the same conclusions, one way or another. I don't have any doubt whatsoever; in seeking a solution, they will follow a path similar to the one I am proposing, because there is no alternative. No one has to be persuaded. I am merely stating what is happening, why it is happening, and what will happen and proposing solutions.

In this case, the ideas, the analyses, and the thoughts I have put forth are the product of reality. They aren't the fruits of imagination or fantasy. Many people in Latin

America have been thinking about this and have reached the same conclusions on their own.

I have felt freer to speak about this topic. I have been referring to this since 1979 — for six years now — and I've been developing these ideas all of that time. I can present them. Our economy has more solid foundations for development. It doesn't depend at all on the United States, which has blockaded us for twenty-six years. It is less dependent on the Western world's economy, and we are less vulnerable to economic pressures and retaliation than the other Latin American countries, which are constantly rescheduling their debts and facing quite serious problems. Their situation isn't the same as ours when expressing these points of view, but I'm convinced that many public figures, many Latin American and Third World politicians, have already reached these conclusions on their own, even though they may not have been in a position to state them as I am doing.

If you read the international wire service reports, for instance, you'll see that in Africa, Nyerere has been speaking out strongly about debt-related problems and Africa's tragic economic situation. He hasn't done this in exactly the same terms, but he is, in essence, reflecting the same concern and the urgent need to seek solutions. That is, we are faced with events and situations in which the countries have no alternative but to find a way out. Any way out that they find will, at least, be in the same direction that I am proposing — maybe not exactly the same thing, but in the same direction. The debt simply cannot be paid. If at one time it was said, "Give me liberty or give me death," today the choice for those governing Latin America is the cancellation of the debt or political death.

We have increased our defense capabilities considerably in the last four years. The people are organized. This has been in response to an open, declared policy of force and threats against Cuba implemented by the U.S. administration.

Jeffrey M. Elliot: The United States and the Soviet Union are presently meeting in Geneva to pursue the subject of arms control. At the same time, the Congress recently approved President Reagan's request for the MX missile program. Do you believe that the president's decision to expand the MX missile program will undermine the present talks in Geneva?

Fidel Castro: The Geneva talks stirred hope throughout the world. But I detect an obvious contradiction in the most recent actions of the United States. I must confess, I also had hopes for those negotiations, because they appeared to signal a more realistic policy on the part of the U.S. government. They might have even signaled the end of the arms race, as well as the end of a U.S. military spending policy which in my judgment will, in the medium term, have disastrous consequences for the entire world.

I think it's absolutely impossible to maintain a $200 billion budget deficit. According to the most recent data, the deficit had already climbed to $20 billion in February. At that rate, it will total $222 billion for 1985. To this must be added the $123 billion trade deficit for 1984. Neither the U.S. economy nor the world economy can hold up under this squandering of resources, because it is well-known that a large part of that money comes from the industrialized countries and, what is worse, from the Third World.

In 1983, the United States took in $40 billion from Europe and Japan, and foreign investment in the U.S. public debt amounted to $170 billion during that period. In this regard, we should look at something that should be alarming for U.S. economists: the fact that the public debt, which took

205 years to reach $1 trillion, increased by $650 billion in the three-year period from 1981 to 1984. I insist that no economy can bear such a burden, and I sincerely believe that the short- and medium-term results are going to be disastrous. It seems to me that in the overall effort to avert the arms race, this objective fact could be an element that would warrant a prudent and realistic approach by the U.S. administration.

I have also noticed that there is a great insistence on the need to step up military programs, such as the MX — which is said to be a tactical question, solely a means of strengthening the U.S. position at the negotiations — and all the other weapons programs. Right now, one can't be sure whether it's a tactical or a strategic question — whether the real intention is to use this program as a bargaining chip in the negotiations, or whether it reflects a determined effort to pursue the arms race in search of military superiority.

Now then, just yesterday two new facts came to light which, in my judgment, will complicate the negotiations. First, the NATO agreement to proceed with the deployment of all the 572 medium-range missiles programmed for Europe. And, second, the NATO agreement to support and participate in the space weapons development program. I think that these are two extremely serious matters. The way I see it, they can't possibly encourage the Soviets to negotiate, and, in the final analysis, it seems that the U.S.'s intransigent refusal to discuss and negotiate a moratorium on the space weapons program will become the key to whether there is détente or not, whether the arms race continues or not.

It would be a mistake to imagine that the Soviets are incapable of matching the United States in this arms race. Of course, they don't want to, but if they are forced to do so, the Soviet people have, on more than one occasion, demonstrated their capacity for enormous sacrifice. During the first half of this century, the Soviets experienced two major foreign interventions. The first took place immediately following the 1917 revolution. The second was the fascist attack in 1941 during World War II, which caused the destruction of thousands of cities and towns and the deaths of 20 million people. You're talking about a people who have known war much more intimately than people in the United States. They do not want war. But there is no doubt that they are capable of making the necessary sacrifices to respond to any challenge, at any cost.

Jeffrey M. Elliot: In the past, both the United States and the Soviet Union have assumed the risks of war. Do you believe that both sides are now determined to take similar risks to achieve peace?

Fidel Castro: I am more familiar with the Soviets, and I know how they feel — both the leaders and the people — about this vitally important question for mankind. I know they are sincere and that they really want to find a peaceful understanding that will reduce the risk of war. Furthermore, this is logical. As I said, they have known war, dramatically, on their own soil. They have more experience and a greater awareness of what war is.

I really feel that, at other times, the leaders of the United States have sincerely sought détente and a decreased danger of war. However, I have my doubts as to whether that is true of the present U.S. administration, and I think there may be some who are really thinking about military superiority.

Jeffrey M. Elliot: In recent years, the U.S. press has reported that Cuba has greatly expanded its domestic defenses. Is this true? Do you fear an armed attack or invasion by the United States?

Fidel Castro: It's no secret that we have increased our defense capabilities considerably in the last four years. Moreover, we have actually revolutionized our ideas about defense. During this period, we have incorporated more than one-and-a-half million men and women into the country's defenses, not counting the army and its reserves. We have trained tens of thousands of cadres. We have prepared for all possible scenarios of aggression against Cuba, even in the most adverse circumstances. And we have gotten the population ready. The people are organized. We are prepared, even in the remotest corners of Cuba, to fight in all circumstances and even under occupation. Why have we done so? Obviously, not as a sport; not for fun or the love of arms. I would have preferred to say, like Hemingway, "farewell to arms." It has been in response to an open, declared policy of force and threats against Cuba implemented by the U.S. administration.

We engaged in this effort even before the present administration took office, when we realized that the wave of conservatism and great economic difficulties in the United States might turn the voters in favor of a chauvinist foreign policy, and that there was a possibility that the Republican Party might win the elections. We were familiar with its program, ideas, and philosophy concerning all Caribbean and Latin American issues. It didn't hide them; it openly proclaimed them in its platform. We perceived a strong ideological component in this administration: the ideas and mentality of crusaders. They virtually proclaimed their objective of sweeping socialism off the face of the earth. In other times, there were people who had similar goals, and we are well aware of the consequences.

The Republican platform, as far as Cuba was concerned, was particularly aggressive. I think that explains and justifies the enormous effort we have made to build up our country's defenses, an effort that was intensified following the U.S. invasion of Grenada. So, what we've done is perfectly logical. We couldn't wait until the U.S. administration decided to invade Cuba to start getting ready. That's a mistake we could not afford to make. Those who have made that error have not survived.

Mervyn M. Dymally: Is the United States directly responsible for Cuba's massive arms build-up or is it — as your critics say — part of a Soviet military build-up in the Caribbean and Latin America?

Fidel Castro: This has nothing whatsoever to do with the Soviet Union. The proof of this is that, for many years, when a relative calm prevailed in the region in regard to Cuba, we did not engage in any special defense effort. But we have done so over the past four years and will continue to do so. Let me state categorically that this effort stems from the threats of the present U.S. administration. We can't forget that Mr. Haig, on numerous occasions, spoke cynically about and repeatedly advocated military actions against Cuba. Thus, these interpretations are absolutely ridiculous and unfounded.

Jeffrey M. Elliot: How would you respond to critics of the Soviet Union who contend that the USSR is both expansionist and warmongering and point to such recent examples as the Soviet invasion of Afghanistan and its efforts to crush the Solidarity movement in Poland? Don't these examples prove that the Soviets are unwilling to abide by international law and to seek peaceful solutions to world conflicts?

Fidel Castro: You can't ask the Soviet Union to remain impassive when it feels threatened. These accusations of warmongering have no historical foundation whatsoever, and any scholar or historian who is familiar with the history of the Soviet revolution knows that is so. Don't forget that the first step following the revolution was intervention; Lenin's first decree, however, was a proclamation of peace — immediately — only twenty-four hours after the victory of the 1917 revolution. The Soviet Union even withdrew from the war, although it meant great concessions and significant territorial losses. It stated and put into effect the right to independence of the nations that made up the old tsarist empire. This fact cannot be ignored. A good example is Finland, which was part of that empire and became an independent nation.

Everyone who has studied history knows that Lenin waged a great battle for the enforcement of that principle; that he acted in keeping with that policy; and that, as a result, several countries which had been part of the empire attained their independence.

We should not forget that the armed actions against the Soviet people came from the West. Even in this, an agreement was reached: the Germans, who attacked and penetrated the Ukraine to Kiev; the French in the south; the English in the Murmansk region in the north; Japan and the United States in the east. Everyone participated. Although World War I had already ended, intervention in the Soviet Union went on for several more years. What transpired later is well known: even Finland itself was used by fascist Germany to attack the Soviet Union. The country was invaded, and contemporary history records no other examples of such massive destruction and death as fascism caused there.

The casualty figures during World War II are well known. For the United States, they totaled some 300,000 dead — I can't tell you the exact figure. In Great Britain, there were also several hundred thousand; in France, the figure was similar. Italy, which participated on the Nazis' side, suffered relatively few casualties. Germany, which started the war, had some 8 million dead; Poland, which was invaded, had 6 million killed — many of whom were exterminated in the concentration camps and gas chambers. Yugoslavia suffered more than 1 million dead. And the Soviet Union sustained over 20 million killed.

The USSR lost nearly as many lives as all other countries in World War II combined. Can such experiences easily be forgotten? Does history show that the Soviet Union was the aggressor or, to the contrary, that the aggressor was the West?

The Federal Republic of Germany is today once again a

big military power. It has U.S. Pershing and cruise missiles in its territory, numerous military facilities, and a massive army. Hitler would truly have envied the Germans' military might and their alliance with the United States.

After World War II, the Soviet Union was surrounded by dozens and dozens of nuclear bases — in Europe; the Middle East; Turkey, which lies on the Soviet border; in the Indian Ocean; in Japan and other Oriental countries — and by military fleets near its coasts in the Mediterranean, the Indian Ocean, and the Pacific Ocean. No one can deny these facts. Encircled by nuclear bombers, nuclear submarines, military bases, spy bases, and electronic installations — the Soviet Union is totally surrounded.

What happened at the end of World War II is perfectly well known. The United States and the USSR were allies. They had an agreement that the Soviets would participate in the war against Japan. Despite its enormous casualties, as soon as the war in Europe ended, the Soviet Union sent troops and military equipment to the Manchurian borders and religiously kept its part of the agreement. However, the United States developed the atomic bomb in absolute secrecy and didn't say a single word about it to the Soviets. The Soviet allies, who had contributed so decisively to the defeat of German fascism, were asked to participate in the war against Japan and yet were never informed about the development of the atomic bomb. History has recorded these facts. They are known and proved.

Consider the Potsdam meeting, for example, in July 1945. There, the United States didn't tell the Soviet Union a single thing about the progress achieved up till then in the development of this weapon. While in Potsdam, Truman received news about the success of the first nuclear test. This matter was even discussed within the U.S. administration. Some officials favored informing the Soviet Union about the bomb — to search for a joint understanding before further development of the bomb after the war.

But this was not to be. The Soviet Union only found out

about the existence of nuclear weapons when the first bombs fell on Hiroshima and Nagasaki — genocide that was totally unjustified from a military standpoint, which can never be glossed over or forgotten. Not only did that action against the civilian population kill hundreds of thousands of people in a matter of seconds, but for many years thereafter, thousands more continued to perish as a result of that ruthless attack, which made guinea pigs of masses of men, women, and children.

How can the Soviet Union be accused of bellicose and aggressive attitudes in the face of these historical realities? How can anyone fail to understand why the USSR is so concerned about everything that happens near its borders? Who is historically responsible for this lack of trust on the part of the Soviets? How can one try to explain international politics so superficially and simplistically?

As long as the U.S. continues to believe that the Sandinista revolution can be defeated by a combination of actions by mercenary bands and economic difficulties, and that the Salvadoran revolutionary movement can be crushed, the U.S. will not be willing to search seriously for negotiated political solutions in Central America.

Mervyn M. Dymally: Let's turn to the issue of Nicaragua. Can the present conflict be resolved through peaceful negotiations? Is a peaceful settlement possible?

Fidel Castro: I'm absolutely convinced that it is — and if the efforts of the Contadora Group have not produced any results, this is simply because the United States does not want peaceful solutions in Central America. Everyone realizes this. The Contadora Group realizes this. All the countries of the world realize this. And, of course, even the government of the United States itself realizes this.

The Contadora Group, after many months of great effort, prepared a very well-balanced draft agreement which — in spite of the great limitations and harsh conditions it imposed on Nicaragua — was accepted by the government of Nicaragua. But it was not accepted by the government of the United States, notwithstanding its repeated promises of support to the Contadora Group. It rejected this draft agreement because of three of its essential points: (1) the prohibition of foreign military bases; (2) the prohibition of military maneuvers; and (3) the withdrawal of military advisers from Central America. In my opinion, these were mere pretexts, because the objective of the U.S. administration in relation to Nicaragua is to crush the Sandinista revolution. In El Salvador, its objective is to exterminate every last revolutionary and to destroy, once and for all, the spirit of rebellion in this Central American people.

As long as the United States continues to believe blindly that the Sandinista revolution can be defeated by a combination of actions by mercenary bands and economic difficulties, and that the Salvadoran revolutionary movement can be crushed, the United States will not be willing to search seriously for negotiated political solutions in Central America. This is my firmest conviction.

Jeffrey M. Elliot: Do you rule out the possibility of direct U.S. military intervention in Nicaragua?

Fidel Castro: No, I don't rule out the possibility. It is obvious that U.S. policy in Central America is leading to a dead end, and there is the risk that when the administration realizes that it cannot achieve its objectives through the mercenary bands, it may find itself in a situation in which there are no other options but to negotiate with or to intervene in Nicaragua.

It is clear that the Reagan administration is obsessive about Nicaragua. To be more precise, the president of the United States has an obsessive attitude about this issue and a very high degree of personal commitment to it. This could lead — at a given moment — to a decision of direct intervention.

It is quite evident that the administration has been preparing for that. It has built eleven new air strips in Honduras and rebuilt and expanded three old ones; it has set up land and sea military installations and training centers and increased its troop strength. Its military exercises and maneuvers are obviously aimed at creating the conditions for an invasion of Nicaragua, if that decision is ever made. It is now possible. Tanks, armored vehicles, and other military equipment — all the military conditions are established.

Of course, at this time, these are being used to pressure Nicaragua. In the future, they can be used as a point of departure for an invasion of that country.

Mervyn M. Dymally: Do you have faith in the Contadora process as a means of resolving the conflict in Nicaragua? If so, do you support the efforts of the Contadora countries?

Fidel Castro: I think so. So far, the Contadora efforts have played an important role in preventing a large-scale war in Central America, and they're now the only hope of preventing a war there.

Cuba welcomes the Contadora efforts, and we've done our best to support them. Recently, I met with the ministers of foreign affairs of Mexico, Colombia, and Panama. I spoke at length with them, and we discussed the situation. We promised them, both publicly and in personal contacts, to extend our utmost support and cooperation.

I do think it's possible to find a negotiated political solution not only for Nicaragua, but also for El Salvador, because we must not forget about El Salvador. The people of that country live in a state of war, which cannot be separated from the peace-related problems in Central America. I believe a solution can also be found there. Let me assure you that I know what the Sandinistas are thinking, what the Salvadoran revolutionaries are thinking. I can assure you that the main obstacle to a negotiated political solution lies in the stubbornness of the United States and its belief that the situation can be solved by force. It's as if the Reagan administration wants to teach an unforgettable lesson, so that nobody in Central or Latin America will ever again think of rebelling against the tyrannies which serve U.S. interests, or against hunger and exploitation. They want to teach a lesson so that nobody really fights for independence and social justice.

Mervyn M. Dymally: Speaking of El Salvador, your critics claim that Cuba is actively working to overthrow the newly-elected government of President Duarte in El Salvador by supplying military arms to the rebels. Is that true?

Fidel Castro: I don't know where this notion of the legal government, of the legality of that government, comes from. Everyone knows that there was a civil war there. Everyone knows that over the last six years, more than 50,000 people have been murdered there by the death squads and by the Salvadoran army itself. Everyone knows that true genocide has been going on there and that

Duarte has contributed to that genocide. Duarte has actually been a coconspirator and an accessory to those crimes and he can't shirk his responsibility for what has been going on there over the last five years.

Everyone knows under what conditions the elections took place: amidst the most ferocious repression, terror, and war. Everyone knows that the electoral campaign was planned by the United States, that the political parties were manipulated by the United States, and that the electoral campaigns were funded by the CIA. They presented this type of election to the people as a way out, as a hope for peace in El Salvador — actually a false hope. They promised the people that there would be peace after the elections, knowing, of course, that the people want peace and are ready to do anything in the search for peace. This was gross and vulgar deceit. It was the road to war — the plan to do away with insurgency — not the road to peace.

The Duarte government and all other allegedly legal bodies are the result of all that manipulation and all those maneuvers by the United States. The revolutionaries never accepted the legality of those elections, because they were really bloodstained elections. They cannot be justified politically or morally. Who are they going to fool now with the alleged legality of the Salvadoran government?

Pinochet, in Chile, could also say that his government is very legal, after the fascist constitution was imposed upon the people in an alleged plebiscite in which no one but he and his constitution took part. And even more so after [U.S. Assistant Secretary of State Langhorne] Motley stated that the West should feel grateful for Allende's overthrow and death. Actually, one can't help wondering how the United States can consider the Salvadoran elections to be legal but the Nicaraguan elections to be absolutely illegal. Despite the fact that the Nicaraguan elections were sabotaged by the United States, the people turned out to vote with enthusiasm, giving the Sandinistas and the left more than 70 percent of the vote. This was witnessed by more than 1,000 observers from around the world: representatives of governments, political organizations and parties, and journalists from everywhere.

At the same time they talk about the legality of the Salvadoran government, they challenge the legality of the Nicaraguan government. I'm not the least bit concerned about charges against Cuba in relation to our solidarity with El Salvador. As I've stated, the United States knows perfectly well that sending weapons to the Salvadoran revolutionaries is very difficult; in practice, almost impossible. But I have no interest whatsoever in clarifying anything on this because I consider that morally, it is absolutely fair to help the Salvadoran revolutionaries. The Salvadoran revolutionaries are fighting for their country; it's not a war from abroad, like the dirty war the CIA carries out in Nicaragua. It's a war born inside the country; one that has been going on for many years. You can't ask the revolutionaries to lay down their arms, to give up fighting and surrender.

I believe the Salvadoran revolutionaries are actually showing great heroism, great fighting capacity, by resisting the huge quantity of weapons sent by the United States — helicopters, airplanes, sophisticated hardware — and the tactics designed by U.S. advisers. They have demonstrated their ability to resist indefinitely. The Salvadoran revolutionaries have, in fact, proved that they can resist indefinitely without receiving any supplies from abroad. We ourselves waged a war against Batista, whose army numbered 70,000. Everyone knows that we waged that war with the weapons we took from Batista's army. I can assure you that, in fact, the main supplier of the Salvadoran revolutionaries is the Pentagon, through the weapons given to the Salvadoran army. That also happened in Vietnam; the revolutionaries seized huge amounts of weapons delivered by the United States to the puppet army.

I really don't know who could feel morally entitled to criticize Cuba for allegedly supplying weapons to the Salvadorans, when the United States admits supplying weapons to the Somozaist mercenaries to overthrow the government of Nicaragua.

Jeffrey M. Elliot: What concrete evidence can you cite to prove your claim that the CIA willfully and maliciously manipulated the Salvadoran elections?

Fidel Castro: The evidence was published in the United States. The CIA admitted it publicly, and I've recently read reports originating in official circles that state how much money was given to each party. It gave money not only to the Christian Democrats but to all the other parties, and it covered the expenses of the election campaign. Proof is not necessary in the face of a confession.

Jeffrey M. Elliot: You have stated, both in this interview and in previous ones, that the crisis in El Salvador poses a more difficult problem than does Nicaragua. Why?

Fidel Castro: I consider that through the actions of the Contadora Group and the draft agreement prepared by them and accepted by Nicaragua, we can see considerable progress in the search for peace with regard to Nicaragua. The formula was clear and within reach; the same cannot be said, however, with regard to El Salvador.

With respect to El Salvador, the Contadora Group has not yet done anything at all. It has concentrated on the situation in Nicaragua — the problem in El Salvador has been ignored. I believe that until the Salvadoran problem is solved, it would be utopian to think that peace has been achieved in Central America. Moreover, objectively, the situation seems much more complicated in El Salvador, since there is greater intransigence from the United States toward accepting negotiations. That is, while the U.S. theoretically accepts the negotiated political formula with respect to Nicaragua, in the case of El Salvador, it absolutely refuses to listen to anything at all about that formula.

The United States has, for years, been implementing a

political and military plan in El Salvador. Formulas would have to be sought that are acceptable to all parties. Undoubtedly, the preparation of this formula would be a very complex task. But even so, I believe that negotiated political solutions can also be found for El Salvador. These are my reasons for saying that it would be more complicated to find a solution in El Salvador, because of these circumstances.

If Maurice Bishop had been alive leading the people, it would have been very difficult for the United States to orchestrate the political aspects of its intervention. Bernard Coard and his group served the U.S., on a silver platter, ideal conditions for the invasion of Grenada.

Mervyn M. Dymally: Let's shift to Grenada. How do you explain the failure of the socialist revolution in Grenada? Was failure inevitable?

Fidel Castro: In effect, what was taking place in Grenada was not a socialist revolution, but a process of social changes. I believe that the basic factor that opened the door — that served the United States a pretext on a silver platter for invading that country, at a lower political price — were the activities of an ambitious and extremist sectarian group. In my view, the main responsibility for the domestic situation created there lies with [Bernard] Coard. An alleged theoretician of the revolution who had been a professor of Marxism in Jamaica, he profited from his reputation as a theoretically well-prepared man and used his reputation as a theoretician to promote his personal ambitions and conspire against Bishop.

This is nothing extraordinary. More than once in the history of revolutionary processes, events of this nature have occurred. The French revolution itself, which later inspired the bourgeoisie all over the world, was full of factional struggles which, in the end, led many, from the most moderate to the most radical, to the guillotine, until the reactionary forces and the eighteenth of Brumaire placed a military strong man in power.

For example, the Kampucheans fought for many years against the puppet army in their country. They even fought against the intervention of the United States, which was secretly participating with its bombers in the struggle to crush the national liberation movement. The Kampucheans waged a truly heroic struggle. I vividly recall the victory of the revolutionary Kampucheans. We received a visit from them; they sent us an emissary — in the person of Ieng Sary. In this very room, where we're now talking, I spoke to Ieng Sary, shortly after the struggle in Kampuchea ended. A well-educated man — undoubtedly he had a Western culture. Always polite, he talked enthusiastically about his revolution. I even introduced him to some other comrades. He left a good impression; no one could have imagined the things he later did together with Pol Pot.

Everyone knows that an extremist spirit prevailed in that process, that the extremist ideas of Pol Pot and Ieng Sary led to inconceivable errors, truly absurd methods. And I'm not referring to the evacuation of the city. In fact, around 4 million people had crowded into the capital, and, in that country without transportation or fuel, it was impossible to support and feed a city of that size. I don't question the possible need to search for a redistribution of the population in order to prevent hunger and produce foodstuffs. There are circumstances in which that can be explained and justified. But the issue lies in the methods used to implement this policy. It's evident that incorrect and extremist methods were used, methods of force, separating families. Moreover, they committed all kinds of crimes in the name of revolutionary ideas. Those were the times of the Cultural Revolution in China and the preeminence of Mao Tse-tung's ideas. They considered themselves proficient disciples of Mao Tse-tung and tried to apply his ideas in their own way, and as a result millions of people died.

There are many people who don't understand. They attribute to this group not revolutionary extremism, but the idea of destroying the country — with the ulterior objective of annexing it to China. There are some who have stated these viewpoints.

But it is not impossible for the disease of extremism to take hold of some people; this often occurs even among petty-bourgeois elements who draw up utopias and try to put them into practice. Unfortunately, there have also been cases of extremism in other revolutionary processes.

In Grenada, however, I don't believe it was an extremist policy on Coard's part. Rather, I think, personal ambition was Coard's basic motivation and what really confused many people in whom he inculcated extremist ideas from supposedly revolutionary positions, as a means of gaining support. In the name of the purity of Marxist-Leninist principles, he portrayed Bishop as a man insufficiently prepared to lead the country. Very subtly, he did it very subtly. He worked in the rank and file of the party, the armed forces, the Ministry of the Interior — always presenting himself as an apostle of the purity of ideas — and astutely, little by little, he created the image of a vacillating, reformist Bishop. Thus, he confused many people of good faith in the revolutionary ranks.

Bishop had great popular support and was well liked by the population. But Coard and his group — who belonged to one of the organizations that joined with Bishop to form the New Jewel Movement — didn't work with the masses. That is, the Coard group didn't work with the masses; it worked among the party members — who were a small group of about 200 — and with the cadres of the army and the Ministry of the Interior. This fifth column, this undermining of Bishop's authority, coalesced at a moment when Bishop — though he had the support of the immense majority of the people — lost the majority within the party, both in the Central Committee and among the membership. This was the fruit of the conspiracy led by Coard and his group. It explains the senseless and mad step of arresting Bishop and, even worse, of firing upon the people and assassinating Bishop. It was that unfortunate event that made it possible for the Reagan administration to perpetrate the cynical and opportunistic invasion of the country.

If Bishop had been alive leading the people, it would have been very difficult for the United States to orchestrate the political aspects of its intervention and bring together that group of Caribbean stooges in a so-called coalition that didn't include a single policeman from the Caribbean — it was exclusively U.S. soldiers. In short, Coard and his group served the United States, on a silver platter, ideal conditions for the invasion of Grenada.

Naturally, they were not going to be met with the people's resistance, for the simple reason that the people were outraged, traumatized by the attitude of this group that had fired upon the people and assassinated Bishop. Thus, a divorce took place; those involved in the coup gathered the weapons of the militia. They disarmed the militia on various pretexts, precisely for fear of the people after what they had done.

This explains the weapons the United States found stockpiled there and that have been used so often in its propaganda and its lies, in its campaigns and in its fabrications, trying to pass off Grenada as a continental subversion center. Despite all that, the United States had no right whatsoever to invade and occupy Grenada; the U.S. had no right to do it.

Obviously, the United States wanted a show of force, some muscle-flexing, to teach a lesson in Grenada. In my view, it committed one of the most inglorious and infamous deeds that a powerful country, such as the United States, could ever commit against a small country. The United States did not really do this in a spirit of justice, or out of solidarity with Bishop, or to punish those responsible for Bishop's death. Rather, it could have been grateful to that irresponsible group. It invaded Grenada to eradicate the revolution and to reestablish the former regime in that country. That's all.

One more thing: the United States invades a country and violates all international laws to do away with a process that was dead. Why? Because I'm totally convinced that Coard and his group committed political suicide. After they assassinated Bishop and fired upon the people, that process could not endure. I believe that it was the people — the people themselves, the Grenadans themselves — who had to solve that problem, and they were going to solve it.

The government could not have endured. We wouldn't have offered any support to that government after it murdered Bishop and fired on the people. After we had assumed that attitude, it would have been difficult for any other socialist or progressive country to support that group, because Bishop actually had great authority and great international prestige. He had attended numerous meetings of the Commonwealth, the Movement of Nonaligned Countries, and the United Nations. The whole world thought highly of Bishop; that Pol Pot-type group that murdered him would never have been forgiven.

As soon as we had finished the airport, we would have left Grenada. We could not leave the airport unfinished; it was a project we had donated to the people of Grenada — one that was useful to them. We might have left only our doctors there, for strictly humanitarian reasons.

Somewhere around here are the dispatches and confidential documents that show everything that happened, as well as the tense relations between us and that group. All cooperation was broken off. Any united defense plan became morally impossible for us. Of course, work on the airport continued. But the messages exchanged, which express our attitude with regard to the events, are in our files. Fearing that they might commit an atrocity, I had urged them not to make the stupid mistake of killing Bishop. But when the people's uprising occurred, they became so frightened and confused that they fired upon the people and shortly thereafter killed Bishop and a group of valuable aides. That is the historical truth.

We fully endorsed Bishop's policies, because they were realistic. They weren't extremist policies. They were based upon the country's situation and its level of development, and they were working for the people's well-being, for Grenada's development. I think the airport would have meant great economic progress for them. Grenada was receiving different kinds of assistance to develop its energy networks, roads, infrastructure, and agricultural production.

Bishop had a program, but not a socialist program — nor could he have had a socialist program. Rather, it was a program for social justice and for the country's development. Bishop implemented an agrarian reform, but he didn't nationalize the hotels. A country that lived on tourism, did not even have its own currency, and had no industries, could not rush headlong into drastic social changes. Bishop was implementing a rational, intelligent program and was really making progress.

I spoke with Bishop when he stopped over in Cuba for the last time, both before and after a trip to several socialist countries. He went there to request credits and equipment for power plants and some light industries, and he returned very pleased. He highly appreciated our cooperation.

Despite everything that happened, the United States had no right to invade that nation. Nor does it even have the right to keep that extremist group in prison or to try them, because no invading force has the right to run the courts and enforce the laws. I think all that is illegal.

What I'm telling you is really our assessment of what happened there. The international dispatches confirm that when the Cuban doctors departed, the country was left without medical care. What purpose has the invasion served?

The whole infamous action was surrounded by all sorts of lies, with no scruples whatever, because the U.S. students on the island never ran any risk. The first thing the coup group did was to give assurances of safety to everyone, and particularly the medical college. The safest people in Grenada were the U.S. students.

It was said a thousand times that it was a military airport, when not a single brick that went into that airport was military. It was being built with the participation of the European Economic Community, the English, the Canadians, and other U.S. allies. How many times was it said that it was a military airport and things like that! That's the shameful and inglorious story.

Those responsible for the situation — those who opened the door for the United States — showed that they weren't really such fanatics and extremists. None of the leaders fought against the U.S. army; what they did was to surrender like cowards. Had they really been revolutionaries, with deep convictions, they would have died fighting the invading forces and would not have surrendered.

That is the sad story and the explanation of the events that enabled the United States to commit its shameful crime in Grenada.

Jeffrey M. Elliot: If your analysis is correct, why did the people of Grenada welcome the Americans with open arms and cheer their presence? Why has the U.S. continued to receive increasing support from the vast majority of Grenadans?

Fidel Castro: I doubt very much that it is receiving increasing support. No, I believe quite the opposite. But, as I explained earlier, the events prior to the invasion facilitated the U.S. demagogy. As I told you, Bishop was a man greatly loved by the people. He was the leader of the Grenadan people. He had the real, sincere, and enthusiastic support of the people. The group involved in the coup plotted against Bishop, arrested him, fired upon the people when they revolted, and, furthermore, assassinated Bishop and other leaders. Naturally, this caused great outrage and confusion among the masses. The United States invaded, insisting that its sole purpose was the noble aim of liberating the country from those people and that it was going to punish Bishop's murderers and those who had fired upon the people. It was logical for a large number of people in that country — even most of the population — to be susceptible to accepting that invasion as desirable.

Just a short time ago — one could say a few years — Grenada had attained independence. There was still no really solid national spirit; that sense of homeland, of nationality, was still in the making. In addition, for people who had been educated in the British traditions of respect for the law, who saw the brutal violations of lawfulness and witnessed the unprecedented events of firing upon the people and the assassination of Bishop, it was logical not to realize what an invasion of their territory by the United States meant for the independence and sovereignty of their country — much less what it entailed for the rest of the Caribbean and for the independence of other peoples. Had this been a country with a strong national awareness, a national spirit already developed, the reaction would have been different, despite their profound outrage over what had happened. With the trauma and the pain left by Bishop's death, the loss of the chief, and the brutality of those involved in the coup, the Grenadan people were in no position to judge the invasion.

Situations such as these show the value of patriotic and national feelings. I believe, for instance, that the people of the United States would not have been pleased with an invasion by a foreign army to rid them of Nixon during the Watergate days. There are many examples of peoples with a strong national awareness. The Saharan people have a strong nationalist, patriotic spirit; the Irish have a high national spirit; the Mexicans have a patriotic and national spirit, which is also very strong; Cuba has it. But you couldn't expect such a spirit from the Grenadans. However, many Grenadan soldiers died fighting heroically against the invaders. Therefore, this argument that the invasion was welcomed with applause is trivial — a really weak and simplistic argument. That does not justify the United States action morally nor does it contribute one iota of dignity to that behavior.

If these were the motives of the U.S. policy, why does it maintain such good relations with the apartheid regime? There, 25 million Africans are being deprived of the most basic rights and brutally oppressed — that is, 250 times the population of Grenada. They don't need U.S. troops to go there and liberate them — they'll see to that themselves. But they would certainly applaud if the United States stopped sending the racists any more investments, technology, or credits; if diplomatic relations were severed; if the U.S. didn't veto UN sanctions against South Africa. This wouldn't cost the blood of a single U.S. soldier.

Now then, what is surprising, what is difficult to explain, what speaks very poorly of the political education of the average U.S. citizen, is the fact that the majority of them could have been so confused, deceived, and led to applaud and support that shameful action by their government.

Public opinion in the United States was manipulated by a pack of lies, told over and over again. U.S. public opinion was manipulated. Melodramatic elements were brought into play: the students kissing U.S. soil on their arrival; the bitterness and frustration resulting from the Vietnam adventure and its humiliating defeat; the problem of the marines killed in Lebanon; and the memory of the Iranian hostage crisis. All of these elements, latent in the spirit of the people of the U.S., were manipulated in a cold, calculated manner in order to justify the inglorious Grenada action.

I believe that history will judge these events, and I have no doubt that some day the people of the United States — or future generations there — will be ashamed of the way the people were manipulated and the lack of political culture and ethics that was shown.

The people can be manipulated; they can even applaud crimes. There are eloquent examples throughout history: when the Nazis annexed Austria, the German people applauded; when the Nazis annexed Czechoslovakia — dismembered and annexed Czechlosovakia — the immense majority of the German people applauded that victory; and when the Nazis invaded Poland, inventing an incident to stage a provocation and unleash the invasion, and when they occupied Warsaw, the vast majority of the German people applauded. Chauvinism, national pride, is nothing new and neither is the possibility of manipulating and deceiving public opinion. So, the applause the Reagan administration may have received for this action means absolutely nothing, in my view. There were people who also applauded at the beginning, when the invasion of Vietnam began; later on we saw the consequences. Ignorant people can be confused by these things: people with political education and sound moral values cannot be so easily deceived.

Mervyn M. Dymally: Given your close relationship with Maurice Bishop — it's said that you looked to him as a brother — why did you not know about the intrigue that went on while Bishop was out of the country? Where did Cuban intelligence break down?

Fidel Castro: I'll explain. It's even more surprising.

Of course we never practice intelligence methods with friendly countries, countries with which we have close relations.

Mervyn M. Dymally: I mean intelligence not in the sense of the CIA, but in the sense of communication. Where did your communication break down?

Fidel Castro: Your question is quite logical; it's absolutely justified. First of all, we do not employ an intelligence apparatus, intelligence bodies, or intelligence methods to gather information about what may be happening in a country with whom we have relations of trust and friendship. There's no methodical and systematic collection of information. We always depend upon the conscious cooperation among revolutionary people, friends, and sympathizers who can explain what's happening within a leadership group, a council of ministers, a central committee. In fact, it's logical for us to have known what was happening in Grenada, since we had very close relations with Bishop and other leaders. In addition to working relations, we were assisting in agriculture, industry, health, education, the army, and even in the Ministry of the Interior. Our ambassador enjoyed excellent relations; so did the party representative, the representative of the Cooperation Committee, the advisers in the army, in the militias, and in the Ministry of the Interior. The truth is, we didn't know about the process that was evolving, and that has been one of our harshest criticisms of those in charge of cooperation with Grenada and our diplomatic representation there.

During that entire period, only one woman comrade from the Federation of Cuban Women — who had been there for a few days on an exchange visit — had written a brief report to her organization on the problems she perceived there. I didn't even hear about the report. It seems no one paid any attention to it.

The wild idea of a split in the country's leadership was inconceivable. What really did happen? The party was made up of a small group of members — some 200. The leadership group was quite small. Coard worked with great subtlety. He did not work openly. He started placing cadre — that is, people from the group that had joined Bishop's party. He did not dissolve that group; he kept it as a faction. Very quietly, and gradually, he placed his sworn followers in key positions in the army, as political instructors, in the Ministry of Security, and in some positions in the party. He had even resigned his position as a member of the Bureau a year earlier as a gesture of selflessness. He went off to a small island and was there playing the role of an isolated man, self-isolated, but he continued being the spiritual guide. That was his style. So, this developed very subtly, very quietly. And Coard gradually gained a majority on the Central Committee — and always in the name of principles.

These methods are always somewhat effective

whenever someone gains a kind of priesthood of the doctrine, guardian of the doctrine, theoretician of the doctrine, philosopher of the doctrine — the one who knows the most about revolutionary doctrine. Although Bishop was an educated man — with great preparation — he was not a professor of Marxism. I tell you this so you will be on your guard with scholars, because they have prestige. [*Laughter*] Let us say: Coard — with Professor Elliot's pardon — was the scholar of politics, the professor of political science; while Bishop was the man who worked with the masses, worked with the people, worked with the administration, and was active internationally. In other words, Coard's conspiracy was carried out quite covertly and subtly. It was not easy to perceive what was in the making.

Now then, there's no doubt that Bishop was very noble and, I'd say more, naive, because he never gave much thought to the problem. He never imagined that a tendency of this type, aimed at isolating him, could develop, and I believe he underestimated the importance of Coard's activities. We have proof of this: several weeks before the events, some questions were being discussed — not the conspiracy, of course. But there had been meetings to analyze the work being done with the workers, the economic work, the work with mass organizations, and the work of the party. These were the matters under discussion. They even made some criticisms of Bishop — they made some critical remarks — but they seemed normal, logical, and even healthy criticisms, which is how Bishop saw them.

We learned some of these things later from the papers published by the U.S. government, which were greatly manipulated. Every day they publish a paper to prove something in a demagogical and dishonest fashion. The invaders seized the records of these meetings. Naturally, we didn't have those records; no party, no political organization, gives the records of its meetings to another organization, no matter how close their ties may be. We keep the records of our party meetings to ourselves. The records of any revolutionary, Marxist, left, or any kind of party are logically not handed over to another party. Besides, these discussions seemed harmless.

The fact is, when Bishop stopped in Cuba on his way to Europe, he spoke with me in the house where he was staying. We talked a lot about the airport under construction, the economic situation, the way projects were going, and ideas for the future. Then Bishop — who had had a meeting several days before his trip — spoke to me self-critically. Sometimes we told him — because we knew it was so — "not enough attention is being paid to the militia — the organization and preparation of the militia." The advisers told us; they explained these things to us. I talked with him about these problems, and he said: "Yes, I've given little attention to the militia. I've given little attention to the work of the party. When I return, I will give more attention to the work of the party and the mass organizations." He even told me about certain ideas for delegating part of his work, distributing his work so that he could have more time for these activities. When he spoke with me, he was candidly self-critical. But almost all the conversation dealt with construction, development projects, road conditions, what he wanted to do with the equipment and the Cuban construction workers when the airport was completed, because it would be finished in a few months. He also spoke about what he would try to obtain in Czechoslovakia and Hungary.

He returned to Cuba and stayed two days. I even took him to see two important works under construction: the Cienfuegos nuclear power plant and the new oil refinery; and we toured the area. The day before he left, we gave an intimate reception in his honor, to which I invited all the comrades in the Political Bureau, the comrade vice presidents of the executive committee of the government, and the ministers who had to do with cooperation in Grenada.

This was all due to the fact that everyone loved Bishop. He was, as you said, a brother — pleasant, friendly, intelligent. People liked meeting him, and we stayed about two or three hours. Almost all the members of the Political Bureau who were at this reception spoke to him.

While Bishop was abroad, those people worked actively in Grenada. A member of Bishop's personal security team even turned out to be one of Coard's sworn men, who informed on the details of the trip. Now, since those problems were already present, they took advantage of Bishop's absence.

When Bishop returned to Cuba, he didn't say a single word about this problem. As I see it, this was for two reasons. First, he underestimated the problem and, second, he may have been embarrassed by the idea of raising an internal problem of his party.

Now, I wonder: if we had known at that time of the discussions which had taken place, could we have done something? Could we have helped to prevent what happened there? Perhaps not. Had he told us that there were problems, he would have conveyed his impression and reduced the issue to something unimportant. We would have listened to him, but nothing more. He himself was not aware of the importance and the potential gravity of the charges, in the form of criticism, that were being addressed to him. But the fact is he went back, and by that time, Coard and his group — who by then had gained control of the majority of the leadership bodies — had already made some major decisions. They decided to leave him as head of the government, but relieve him of his responsibilities as head of the party. When Bishop arrived at the Grenada airport, Coard was not there to welcome him, as was usual. Practically no one was there to welcome him. A short time later — within a few days — there was a meeting, and he was now in an obvious minority. He was already in a minority in the party leadership! Events rushed ahead.

It might have been possible to do something if the gravity of the problem had been known two months earlier — perhaps a month before the events — and some delegation of ours could have talked with them. It's possible that we might have been able to do something to avert the catastrophic outcome. But no one can guarantee this. Coard's conspiracy, his intrigues, and his demagogic behavior had already undermined Bishop's authority within the party almost irreversibly. But Bishop was a noble man who was capable of any sacrifice to help his country. The new majority must have known that it needed at least his cooperation to move forward. Nevertheless, nothing that fox Coard did was sane, sensible, or reasonable.

How did Coard's group interpret Bishop's stopover in Cuba on his return? I had asked him to stay for two days. How did they interpret the tour we made and the reception we gave for him, where almost all the leadership of the party was present? Their interpretation was that Bishop had informed us of their internal problems and that the attention offered him in Cuba was an expression of support for Bishop. So, the first charge they made against him was that during his trip Bishop had informed other parties of the internal situation in Grenada. That was the first charge made by this factional, conspiring group. A few days later, Bishop went to our embassy in Grenada and explained that there were problems — he said clearly then that there were problems. He said he feared, he was worried, that they might even attempt to assassinate him. But he said he thought he would solve the difficulties, that he could solve them.

Almost immediately, the conspirators launched another charge against Bishop. They accused him of slandering Coard, of gross defamation, of spreading the rumor that Coard wanted to assassinate him. That was the most serious charge against him, and the events were triggered almost immediately. As a matter of fact, Bishop did consider the possibility that there might be an attempt to eliminate him physically. The events proved dramatically that he was absolutely correct — that these people were capable of murder. Bishop may have mentioned his concerns to several people. A meeting took place to analyze the charge of slandering Coard. One of Bishop's personal security guards — actually, one of Coard's men — testified that Bishop had given him instructions to spread that rumor. That was when they took Bishop into custody and placed him under house arrest. That's the origin of his arrest.

Now then, the situation for us was delicate. We couldn't meddle in the problem. First, as a rule, we adopt the principle of noninterference in the internal affairs of any country with which we are cooperating. This rule is strictly observed. We contribute to unity and help resolve this type of problem if the parties involved request our cooperation. No matter how much we liked Bishop, we couldn't have violated this principle. In fact, it was Bishop who asked that the Cuban construction personnel have weapons. They were not to be used in internal conflicts, but only in case Gairy and the CIA organized a mercenary expedition and the revolutionary forces needed help. The Cuban construction personnel had only infantry weapons; they were not supposed to fight against the U.S. Army. They didn't even have an "Arrow" [an antiaircraft rocket launcher] to shoot down the airplanes and helicopters. It was on Bishop's request and insistence that the airport construction personnel received weapons. But Bishop wasn't contemplating a U.S. invasion — rather, a mercenary invasion, a dirty war, a Bay of Pigs–type invasion. To fight against U.S. troops would have called for a different type of personnel, different weapons, and a different kind of war. Above all, there would have had to be a government worth defending, one supported by the people.

When the internal conflicts erupted, we adopted a policy of not getting involved in any way. First, because, as I said, it is our rule. Second, because there was no legal basis to justify giving support to Bishop. A decision to relieve him of his position in the leadership of the party could not be challenged, because it had been adopted by a majority. In this case, the conspiracy assumed "democratic forms"; they had achieved a majority within the leadership group. Third, any action on our part would have provoked armed clashes between the Cuban personnel and the Grenadan soldiers, whose command was controlled by the Coard group. That would certainly have given the United States a perfect pretext for its intervention: a war between Cuban and Grenadan personnel.

When the people's uprising took place, and Bishop was taken out of prison, one of Bishop's comrades went to the embassy to seek our support. A wire was sent to Havana saying that Bishop was asking for support from the armed Cuban personnel in the construction brigade. The wire was accompanied by public reports on the repression, the people's demonstration, and Bishop's assassination.

Frankly, it would have been a serious political mistake to have authorized the Cuban personnel to become involved in the Grenadan revolutionaries' domestic troubles. Bloody combat would have ensued, and, even if things had turned out in Bishop's favor and the U.S. intervention hadn't occurred, Bishop would have had to rule the country without his party, without the army, without the police and security units, and without the revolutionary cadres. Coard had gained control of those institutions, and many of their members believed — almost blindly — that they were serving the revolution. It was an absurd situation. I would never, under any circumstances, have authorized the Cuban personnel to have become involved. Of that you can be sure. Our answer would have been "No." But there wasn't even time to answer; there was no need to answer.

Our relations with the coup group were very bad throughout the crisis and even worse after they fired upon the people and killed Bishop. When we learned that they had made those accusations against Bishop, I immediately made it clear that Bishop hadn't said anything at all to us concerning the existing problems when he stopped over in Cuba. And I also made it clear that we hadn't interfered — nor ever would — in their domestic affairs. Several messages were exchanged. Ours were quite harsh and critical. We were really indignant. We hadn't even issued an official statement, as we were waiting for the situation to become clear. When Bishop's assassination was reported, we issued a very harsh statement, making it clear that our political relations with the new leaders of Grenada would have to undergo profound and serious analysis.

What kept us from withdrawing? We might have had to withdraw in a week, in view of the tenseness of the relations between us. What kept us from doing so was the news that U.S. intervention forces were sailing toward Grenada. That was the one moment when we couldn't withdraw from the country. And that's the objective truth. We can prove it, because we have all the messages they sent us and the ones we sent them.

We are the ones who maintained the clearest position. We have told the truth about everything that happened there. Some people in the United States have recognized this. For example, when it was reported that there were 2,000 Cubans in Grenada, we said that there were exactly 784, including the diplomats and their families, so many construction workers, and so many advisers. We gave all the exact figures; we published everything. We never told a falsehood — not even a tiny one — about the situation in Grenada. Naturally, the people of the U.S. didn't learn about this; they had no way of doing so. They simply heard the lies that the U.S. administration fed them. No one informed them about what was happening. I'm giving you a full account of the events as they actually happened.

If the creditors insist on collecting the debt, if they implement the IMF measures against the people, and if a solution isn't found for the economic crisis, there will be widespread revolutionary outbreaks throughout Latin America.

Jeffrey M. Elliot: In recent statements, you've described Latin America as a potential powder keg. Why? Does the future hold in store an explosion?

Fidel Castro: I have no doubts in my mind that will be the case if the problem of the foreign debt isn't solved. This can be demonstrated mathematically. An enormous socioeconomic crisis has been gradually developing in Latin America; it's the most serious crisis in all its history — much more serious than the crisis of the 1930s.

Latin America's population is now three to four times larger than it was in the 1930s, and the social problems have piled up. The purchasing power of Latin American exports has dropped.

At the time of the Alliance for Progress — after the Cuban revolution and precisely due to the fear that new revolutionary processes would appear in Latin America — Kennedy launched the Alliance for Progress. It was based on the need to effect social changes: agrarian reforms, tax reforms, etc. For the first time, the idea of agrarian reform met with acceptance in the United States. Until then, any government that proclaimed the need for an agrarian reform or carried one out was considered "communist." This was the case of the agrarian reforms in Guatemala and Cuba. Eisenhower, at Nixon's instigation, began to organize the Playa Girón expedition immediately after we carried out the agrarian reform in 1959. The Alliance for Progress — proclaimed at the time of the Playa Girón mercenary invasion of Cuba — advocated agrarian reform, tax reform, social development, and a better distribution of national income. This was all based on a $20 billion investment to be made over a period of ten to fifteen years. That is, the ideas for some social changes were accompanied by a $20 billion pledge for economic cooperation.

Twenty-four years have since passed, and there have been no such agrarian reforms, save for one exception: the one in Peru, which was carried out by the military government. There were no agrarian reforms anywhere else, no tax reforms, and no equitable income redistributions. Since then, the population has doubled; social problems have multiplied; shantytowns have mushroomed; and unemployment has soared. In addition, there is an international economic crisis. The area's export products have less purchasing power than in the 1930s and the countries have an enormous debt. This will force them to pay $40 billion a year for the next ten years — $400 billion in ten years — just in interest. This is twice as much money, every year, as Kennedy had proposed for aid over a longer period, and, in ten years, twenty times as much as the aid Kennedy offered.

This is compounded by a deterioration in the terms of trade amounting to $20 billion; the flight of capital caused by the overvaluation of the dollar; high interest rates; and staggering inflation in Latin America — which went up to around 130 percent for the area in 1983. In 1984, it reached 175 percent. Naturally, all this fosters the flight of foreign currency. The people lose confidence in their own currencies and those with money exchange it for dollars and deposit them in U.S. banks. Reagan then uses the money that's been deposited in U.S. banks for his "star wars" program and for the arms race.

During past centuries, colonialism never plundered the colonized countries to this extent. The fact is, the poor and needy countries are financing the economies of the United States and the rest of the industrialized world. All of this now coincides with a democratic opening. Reagan says that democracy is advancing in Latin America — he practically claims credit for this. I say that what's advancing is the crisis. The military are washing their hands of state administration because, in the midst of this deep

socioeconomic crisis, these countries are becoming unmanageable — which is one of the reasons for the process
of democratic openings.

Now then, if these countries are forced to pay this debt
under the present crisis conditions and with the attendant
factors I have explained — if the International Monetary
Fund's measures are implemented — they're going to ruin
the process of democratic openings and create really explosive social situations. The people are no longer in a position to tolerate greater sacrifices and restrictions, as has already been shown in three countries. In the Dominican Republic — a more or less stable country — immediately following the implementation of the first of the International
Monetary Fund's measures, a spontaneous rebellion, an
uprising of the people, resulted. The army and the police
had to be sent into the streets, where they killed dozens of
people and wounded hundreds more, all of which totally
discredited the government and created a very tense situation. In Panama, just a few measures aimed at balancing
the budget brought hundreds of thousands of people into
the streets. Bolivia is practically paralyzed. According to
the latest figures, inflation was 2,300 percent last year.

The new governments that have appeared in Argentina,
Uruguay, and Brazil — with the democratic openings and
the people's support — cannot send the army and the
police to fire upon the people. The people are becoming
aware of this, and their state of mind is vastly different
from anything I've ever seen. It's something new — a state
of mind unlike anything I've seen in the past twenty-six
years of revolution. I anticipate that, if the creditors insist
on collecting the debt, if they implement these measures
against the people, and if a solution isn't found for the economic crisis, there will be widespread revolutionary outbreaks throughout Latin America. There will, of course, be
exceptions, as there are to any rule, but I think the present
situation is really critical, really serious. I haven't the
slightest doubt about what I'm saying.

Mervyn M. Dymally: What can and should the United States do to prevent this powder keg from erupting into a egional war between the Latin American nations and the United States?

Fidel Castro: I think very few countries are likely to support the United States in that hypothetical struggle, which will possibly not take the form of an overt war in the military sense but will indeed bring about serious political and economic conflicts with unforeseeable consequences. That is because their memories of what happened in the Malvinas [Falkland Islands] are still fresh. During the Malvinas War, nearly all Latin American countries gave Argentina their full support, even though it had an indefensible, isolated, and discredited government. The war contributed to the deterioration of relations between the United States and Latin America, because Latin Americans could see the contempt with which they were treated. Despite the Organization of American States and all the agreements and hemispheric treaties, the United States sided with a European country in a war against a Latin American nation. That Latin American solidarity was the result of emotional public opinion; economic interests were not involved.

The economic crisis and the huge debt, however, are problems that affect all Latin American countries without exception and will generate considerable unity. The economic and foreign debt crises can give rise to conflicts. These are completely new factors, whose combined effects have never been felt in the history of this hemisphere. I think that the Latin American societies will explode if these problems aren't solved.

I think that the Latin American countries are going to unite to try to find a negotiated solution for the problem of their debts and for these economic problems. I believe that the two key factors are strict implementation of the principle of nonintervention in the internal affairs of the Latin American countries and the development of economic relations on a different basis from that which presently exists. The latter may be expressed more concretely in the cancellation of the debt and the elimination of those factors that generate unequal terms of trade. These unequal terms of trade are a kind of law, a historical tendency that has gone on year after year: high interest rates; the overvaluation of the dollar; monetary policies that are implemented at the expense of the economies of the Third World countries; protectionist measures; and the dumping of subsidized products by the industrialized world.

For example, whereas the European Economic Community used to import large amounts of sugar, it now exports considerable quantities of sugar, thus bringing prices down. It exports subsidized meat, which also brings down those prices. The same thing has happened in the United States: its sugar imports have been cut back drastically, thereby reducing the incomes of dozens of Third World countries. This has all occurred in the midst of this crisis, when they're being charged staggering interest and are faced with the implementation of protectionist measures against Latin America's textile, steel, and other exports. Despite friendly words and good intentions, these conditions — which amount to extortion and the exploitation of an entire continent — will trigger a very serious political crisis. That's what I think.

Mervyn M. Dymally: In your previous answer, you discussed the debt of several Latin American countries. You did not, however, discuss Cuba's debt. It's widely reported that you are heavily in debt to the Soviet Union. Is that correct? If so, how do you expect to repay this debt?

Fidel Castro: As I've explained, Cuba's hard currency debt is the smallest in Latin America — something like $300 per capita. The debt which Cuba, as a developing country in need of credits for investment, has contracted with the other socialist countries does not, in practice, imply any kind of problem. There are two reasons for this.

First, the prices we get from all the socialist countries are fair, entirely satisfactory to us, and are guaranteed against unequal terms of trade and the relative deterioration of the prices of our export products. If the prices of our imports rise, so do the prices of our exports. We do not suffer from protectionist measures or dumping by the socialist countries.

Second, we have never had any financial difficulties with the other socialist countries. Our debt is rescheduled with a ten-, fifteen-, or even twenty-year grace period, without interest. What we are advocating is that the economic relations between the industrialized capitalist countries and the Third World countries be patterned after the economic relations we enjoy with the rest of the socialist community. If those formulas were implemented, the difficulties would be overcome.

Apartheid is the most shameful, traumatizing, and inconceivable crime that exists in today's world. I can't think of anything else as serious — from a moral and human standpoint — as apartheid. The survival of apartheid is a disgrace to humanity.

Jeffrey M. Elliot: In recent months, South Africa's system of racial apartheid has drawn considerable criticism. Most nations in the world have struggled long and hard against the problem of apartheid. Do you envisage an end to apartheid? If so, how?

Fidel Castro: Indeed, everyone has spoken about apartheid, and resolutions on this problem have been adopted at the United Nations. But it cannot be said that most of the world has struggled against apartheid.

My view is that the United States and the major European industrialized countries are responsible for the survival of apartheid. That is because, in fact, their struggle has come down to statements, phrases, words, and some votes in the United Nations.

Apartheid is the most shameful, traumatizing, and inconceivable crime that exists in today's contemporary world. I can't think of anything else as serious — from a moral and human standpoint — as apartheid. Particularly after the struggle against Nazi fascism, after the independence of the former colonies, the survival of apartheid is a disgrace to humanity. However, the major industrialized countries — the United States included — have made heavy investments in South Africa and collaborated with the apartheid regime — economically, technologically, and through the supply of weapons. In fact, South Africa is an ally of the West, and it is the West that has actually made it possible for that system to endure.

South Africa has scorned world public opinion. Not only has it resisted any changes in the system and snubbed all United Nations' resolutions, but it has even refused to grant independence to Namibia. Not a single, effective, practical measure has been adopted against South Africa, really pressuring it to put an end to the apartheid system. The United States has systematically opposed all sanctions against the South African regime.

As long as South Africa continues to receive technological, economic, and military assistance, it will remain unaltered, adamant, and continue its blackmailing position. South Africa, like Pinochet, the West's other fascist ally, parades itself before the West as the great standard-bearer of anticommunism and opponent of social changes.

I wonder: Is there any fascist regime in the last forty years that has not been an ally of the United States? In Spain, the Franco regime; in Portugal, the Salazar regime; in South Korea, the fascist military; in Central America, Somoza, the military dictatorships in Guatemala and El Salvador; in South America, Stroessner and the military dictatorships in Argentina, Uruguay, and Brazil; the Duvalier regime in the Caribbean. I don't know of any reactionary, fascist state that has not been a close ally of the United States.

The West is responsible for the survival of apartheid.

How can you justify the aggressive, subversive measures against Nicaragua and the economic blockade of Cuba — which has already lasted twenty-six years — and then talk about constructive relations with the apartheid regime? If, in compliance with the universal condemnation of apartheid, South Africa were effectively isolated, economic sanctions were implemented against it, and everyone were to support them, South Africa's apartheid system would come to an end.

The measures taken against revolutionary countries, the retaliation against countries which adopt a socialist option, are not taken against apartheid. Nothing about apartheid has produced sufficient revulsion in the leaders of the Western countries; just embarrassing — simply embarrassing — situations, which they try to justify with hypocritical statements.

I'm not saying that an international war should be

waged against South Africa; I'm not saying that violent measures should be taken. They're not needed. What is needed is simple international pressure: political, moral, technological, and economic. This will not harm in the least the vast majority of South Africa's population, who live in the ghettos and are being massacred and assassinated daily. Not a month goes by without a slaughter of greater or lesser magnitude.

I believe that the adoption of measures to pressure the racist, fascist, arrogant, and insolent minority in South Africa would be welcomed by all Third World countries and by world public opinion everywhere, without exception. Not a single country would defend South Africa, not even Israel, which cooperates with the South African government, because it is the most discredited cause in the world today. As long as this is not done, South Africa will continue to flout world public opinion; it will continue to snub the international community.

Jeffrey M. Elliot: Your critics contend that Cuba has adopted an adventurist foreign policy, as illustrated by your military presence in Angola and Ethiopia. How can Cuba's actions in these two countries be justified?

Fidel Castro: We sent troops outside our country for the first time in 1975, precisely when South Africa invaded Angola at the moment of its independence. We are the only country which has actually fought the South African racists and fascists — the only country in the world — in addition to Angola, of course, which was under attack.

You can be absolutely sure that all African countries have always admired and been thankful for this action by Cuba. That aggression is what motivated us to send troops to Angola — to fight the South Africans.

That commitment dates back more than twenty years, to our aid to the former Portuguese colonies' struggle for independence: Angola, Cape Verde, Guinea-Bissau. In international organizations and in practice, we have always supported the struggle for the liberation of those countries, because, along with Mozambique, they were the last European colonies in Africa. For more than fifteen years, we helped the MPLA [Movimento Popular de Libertação de Angola — People's Movement for the Liberation of Angola] and, when the country was just about to assume self-government, the CIA and the South African government intervened to wipe out the MPLA. Some people wanted to gain control of the oil in Cabinda, and the South Africans wanted to prevent a progressive movement like the MPLA from coming to power. Initially, we had not employed troops. We had sent a number of weapons and advisers to four points in Angola: one in the southern region, in the area of Benguela; a second in the central region; a third in the vicinity of Luanda; and a fourth in Cabinda. That is, groups of advisers — several hundred — went there to train the MPLA fighters, and a small number of weapons were sent.

The South Africans had already invaded the southern part of Angola's territory. The Portuguese, out of political cowardice, tolerated it. Later, just prior to independence day, the South Africans launched an in-depth attack, and Zairian troops attacked the north — in the direction of Luanda — and Cabinda in an attempt to seize its oil deposits. Angola was to be partitioned.

When these attacks occurred, the South African troops — who advanced over 300 kilometers inside Angolan territory — ran into one of the training centers, where there were a few dozen Cuban instructors and a few hundred Angolans. The South Africans attacked the training center with artillery and armored vehicles. The Cubans and the Angolans fought back and it was there that the first Cubans died.

The South Africans continued to advance. At that moment, their allies, the Zairian troops, approached Luanda from the north and attacked Cabinda. After the South Africans clashed with the Cuban instructors and their Angolan trainees, they continued to advance at full speed. It was then that we decided to airlift a special battalion to try to stop the continued South African march. The Cuban battalion took up position alongside the Angolans at various points along a line to the north of a natural barrier, the Queve River. They blew up the bridges and dug in.

However, when those forces arrived at one of the major roads, the Huambo-Luanda highway, they found that the South Africans had already crossed the river. They had to set up their defense lines between Luanda and the Queve River on the outskirts of a town called Quibala. Using natural defenses and fortifications, they stopped the South Africans from reaching Luanda.

The offensive against Luanda from the north was also beaten, as was the one against Cabinda. If my memory doesn't fail me, all of this happened in November 1975.

The South Africans were there. They held more than half of Angola's territory, and we had only one unit when that situation broke out. There was no choice but to send more troops, since that unit could not be left there, alone and isolated. So, new infantry units, tanks, and artillery were dispatched. When the South Africans clashed with those forces, they began to retreat and were pushed back to the Namibian border.

This is the true story and the reason why those troops were sent to Angola and why they have had to remain there — from the time of the South African occupation of Namibia and its aggressive actions against the southern part of Angola.

The purpose of those troops is basically to defend Angola against a large-scale, in-depth attack. Their mission is to defend the main points along a strategic line leading to the south of Angola, so that the 1975 operation cannot be repeated.

That is their main task, besides defending the region of Cabinda, with its oil deposits — oil is Angola's major resource. Cabinda is of great importance.

There are also units stationed in central Angola that may be deployed north or south if the 1975 situation repeats itself.

This wasn't a drawn-up plan, but a situation that cropped up — an unforeseen, unexpected situation. Little did we think that South Africa, considering its international disrepute, would dare launch its troops against Angola, an African country which had just won its independence and had international sympathy and solidarity. For this very same reason, our troops have had to remain in Angola for nearly ten years.

Let me correct myself: the first time we sent military personnel to Africa — not black Africa — was shortly after the victory of the Cuban revolution. Algeria, which had become independent, was attacked by Morocco, which sought to take over part of that nation's territory. The situation was quite similar to the one I've just mentioned. We had had very good relations with the Algerians for many years, during their struggle for independence against the French army. When they triumphed and the French troops withdrew, a situation similar to that of Angola developed. In fact, that was the first time Cuban troops were dispatched abroad. Morocco wanted to take over the Algerian iron ore deposits located close to its border. Similarly, when the Spaniards withdrew, Morocco later invaded Western Sahara, in order to seize the phosphorus. At that time, our aid to the Algerians was very important, because it helped in starting negotiations and reaching an agreement between Algeria and Morocco.

Ethiopia was the third African country where Cuban military personnel were sent. Until very recently, Ethiopia had lived under a feudal regime. Before the revolution, there was even slavery in Ethiopia. We appreciate the importance of the revolution in Ethiopia, which is one of the largest African countries, and which has a long tradition of independence. Ethiopia is a very poor country — one of the poorest in Africa. Right after the revolution, contacts were established between [Haile] Mengistu and the Ethiopian leaders and ourselves.

In fact, we were among the first to establish relations with Ethiopia and were their advocates before the socialist countries. We also sent them doctors, teachers, weapons, and, here again, history repeated itself. On that occasion, the apple of discord was the Ogaden and its potential oil deposits. An invasion from the south — from Somalia — was launched to seize the Ogaden, a huge area of Ethiopian territory, while the separatist movement in the north was being fanned with the aid of countries such as the Sudan, Saudi Arabia, and others.

It was a difficult moment for Ethiopia. The revolution could have collapsed; the Ethiopian people needed our help and we sent it. No one could help them when they were invaded by Mussolini's troops, but this time they received support from tiny Cuba.

The case of Ethiopia, however, is quite different from that of Angola, a country which became independent after more than 400 years of colonial rule. There, skilled-labor jobs were monopolized by the Portuguese, while nothing but semislave work was reserved for the native population. A big country, Ethiopia has a population of 35 million and a long-standing tradition of independence, organization, self-administration, and military experience. They are a people with a fighting tradition. The Ethiopians are great fighters — excellent, courageous, determined soldiers. By the way, the Angolans have only been able to develop these virtues considerably since their recent independence. The essential thing for Ethiopia was to survive at that difficult moment, and we helped them. Afterward, they were able to develop, in a short period of time, their enormous human potential for defense.

In Ethiopia, our military presence is less decisive, less important. It has decreased gradually, and only a few well-equipped units with combat capabilities still remain. But compared to Ethiopia's total forces, they are more of a symbol of our solidarity. They will remain there as long as the Ethiopian government deems it advantageous.

That is not the situation in Angola — a country with a smaller population, less experience, and faced with South Africa's military might. There, too, the dirty war was organized through the South Africans, who did just what the United States is doing in Nicaragua. They're doing the same in Angola and Mozambique. Many countries of black Africa feel threatened by that policy.

There were no counterrevolutionary bands in Mozambique. They were organized by South Africa, with former policemen and soldiers who had served under the Portuguese or under Ian Smith in former Rhodesia. They have created very serious problems for Mozambique.

In Angola, UNITA [União Nacional para Independência Total de Angola] — a Portuguese creation and later an ally of South Africa — already existed. They have also waged a dirty war and created difficulties. So, Angola is faced with two threats: the counterrevolutionary bands and the South African threat.

In each of the three situations where we sent combat personnel, there were, indeed, powerful motivations. I believe that these three causes cannot be challenged: the integrity of Algeria, the integrity and independence of Angola, and the integrity of Ethiopia and the survival of the most just of revolutions in a feudal and slave state. I consider these to be three truly honorable causes. In fact, I would say that they are among the most honorable ones in the history of Africa.

Mervyn M. Dymally: How do you view the situation in Namibia? What will the future hold?

Fidel Castro: Indeed, Namibia is part of all this. It is a very just liberation movement. So were the struggles in Zimbabwe and Mozambique that I mentioned earlier. We have aided the liberation movements in Africa to the extent possible. We were able to offer Mozambique little assistance, since we really had no place from which to help them. They received a lot of support from Tanzania, which played a prominent role in assisting the liberation movements in Africa. I would say that Tanzania has played a most honorable and prominent role in Africa. Julius Nyerere is one of the worthiest and most meritorious historical figures in that continent.

We were able to help Angola through the Congo. We helped Guinea-Bissau in its struggle for independence through the Republic of Guinea, when Sékou Touré was alive; we helped in the training of cadres and supplied them with weapons and advisers. There were some Cubans in Guinea-Bissau at that time, but there were no troops. The three cases in which we sent troops were Algeria, Angola, and Ethiopia. In Algeria, we did so during the early years of the revolution — over twenty years ago; in the case of Angola, almost ten years ago; and in Ethiopia, some seven years ago.

In the Horn of Africa, we did our best to avert the war between Somalia and Ethiopia. Mengistu, Siad Barre, the president of South Yemen, and I had a meeting in Aden. Our discussions lasted for many hours. Siad Barre pledged not to attack Ethiopia, but, unfortunately, he got carried away by territorial ambitions, chauvinistic feelings, and political opportunism. He thought Ethiopia was weak at that moment and attacked with all his forces.

Who pushed him and why to undertake such an action are matters which should be investigated. I don't want to make any unfounded accusations. I only want to put on record that today he is a great ally of the United States.

These are the situations where we have been involved. We withdrew from Algeria after a short period, and we don't intend to remain in Angola or Ethiopia forever. Our mutual understanding is that once these countries no longer need our aid, we will withdraw. This will be decided by the countries themselves. The Ethiopians believe it is still necessary for some units to remain; the Angolans also consider that they need the troops there for the time being. There is no national or economic interest. I can tell you that our actions have been inspired by feelings of solidarity, by the purest internationalist spirit. No one would feel a greater satisfaction than our country once our troops are no longer required.

However, we will not desert them. We will not leave them on their own, as long as they feel that our assistance is needed. That will be their decision, not ours.

In the case of Namibia, it must be included among the great and just causes of Africa. Namibia has fought tenaciously: thousands of its courageous sons and daughters have died there. Its civilian population, which has taken refuge in Angola, has been the victim of brutal South African massacres. But the West never even hears anything about this.

In brief, I think that nothing can stop the course of history. Nothing can prevent Namibia's independence, just as nothing can prevent the tens of millions of Africans living in ghettos and Bantustans in their own homeland from some day becoming the masters of their own destiny. The concentration camps of Dachau and Auschwitz also came to an end one day.

Mervyn M. Dymally: Given Cuba's stated commitment to the principles of liberation and self-determination, how can you justify the presence of Russian troops in Afghanistan? Isn't the Russian invasion of Afghanistan an embarrassment to independent socialist countries?

Fidel Castro: I have discussed the problem of Afghanistan in several previous interviews. Let me tell you one thing: the West must bear a large share of the responsibility for the situation in Afghanistan.

Afghanistan is one of the most backward countries in the world. A feudal regime existed there until April 1978. It had an illiteracy rate of 80 percent and an infant mortality rate of 235 for every 1,000 live births — one of the highest in the world. Two thousand families owned nearly 70 percent of the land, and the Afghan population consisted of around 1,500 tribes.

I believe that Afghanistan was one of those places in the world where a revolution was becoming more and more necessary. As soon as that revolution took place — as it inevitably had to — CIA activities began, subversive activities exactly like those now being carried out in Nicaragua. The United States has invested $1 billion in helping the counterrevolutionary bands since the beginning of that revolution.

The Afghan revolution led to a series of tensions in the region. Starting in 1978, problems began to arise along its border with Pakistan, as did tensions with Iran — a country in which a revolution had taken place, for similar reasons. We sent Cuba's foreign minister to visit Pakistan and Afghanistan to try to find some formula of understanding between Afghanistan and its neighbors. In September 1979, the Sixth Summit Meeting of Nonaligned Countries was held in Havana. I met individually with [Muhammad] Zia ul-Haq, the president of Pakistan; the then-president of Afghanistan, [Noor Mohammad] Taraki; and the foreign minister of Iran — all member countries of the Nonaligned Movement. In addition, I managed to arrange a meeting in Havana of the leaders of the three countries, in order to find solutions for the problems of that region. The meeting was held and was quite satisfactory.

Unfortunately, while Taraki was in Havana — for a week or so, I think — a sectarian group conspired against him. A few days later, there was a palace coup — similar to the one in Grenada. This ended in his death — his murder — and the ascension to power of [Hafizullah] Amin, who resembles Pol Pot. I had met Amin after the triumph of the Afghan revolution. You can't imagine what a pleasant man he was! Exactly like Ieng Sary, who, as I told you, also visited Cuba following the revolution in Kampuchea. I've had the rare privilege of meeting some figures who were extremely courteous, well-educated, with a Western background, and who had studied in Europe or the United States, only to find out that they later did horrible things. It's as if, at a given moment, people go mad. It seems that there are people whose brain neurons aren't adapted to the complexities of revolutionary political problems, so they do crazy things that are quite amazing.

Everyone had a hand in that situation until the events that took place in Afghanistan in late 1979. True, the Soviets were helping the Afghans, but that is because Taraki requested their help. Amin also requested Soviet help. There were many Soviets there, who assisted in a wide range of fields — military, economic, and technical — until Soviet troops were sent into the country on a massive scale.

Revolutions always entail more than a few complications and headaches, essentially as a result of counterrevolutionary actions fostered from abroad. No revolution has ever escaped these problems. Not the French revolution of 1789, the Soviet revolution of 1917, the Chinese, Vietnamese, Cuban, or Nicaraguan revolutions. There are no exceptions. These problems inevitably arise from attempts promoted from abroad to overthrow the revolution. This, in fact, is what occurred in Afghanistan. An extremely complicated situation was created.

I think that wherever problems and tensions anywhere threaten peace — as in Central America, southern Africa, and the Middle East — you must try to find political solutions, so that peace can be achieved with honor and justice. Several countries are interested in finding a peaceful solution to the problems of the region. I think the Iranians are interested in finding a solution, as is Pakistan. The Muslim countries also want to find a solution. I think that the Soviets are likewise interested in finding a solution, because of their proximity to the area — they share a border with Afghanistan. The CIA, of course, has interests in Afghanistan, as in all countries, and it's doing everything possible to create problems for the Afghan government and the Soviets. It's pouring enormous quantities of weapons and money into that country, using the émigrés, playing upon the political backwardness of a segment of the Afghan people, and exploiting religious fanaticism in order to create problems for the Afghan revolutionaries and the Soviets. I don't think the CIA is particularly interested in promoting peace in the area.

If I were asked, I'd advocate trying to find a peaceful solution based on respect for Afghanistan's right to its sovereignty and its revolution.

I sincerely believe that the Afghan revolution was both just and necessary. We could support nothing that would jeopardize the Afghan revolution. We sympathize with and support the Afghan revolution. I say this frankly. I think Afghanistan can be a nonaligned country, but one where the revolutionary regime is maintained. If a solution is sought that is based on the idea that Afghanistan should go back to the old regime and sacrifice the revolution, then, unfortunately, I don't think there will be peace there for a long time.

I know the Afghans. One of the characteristics of that country is that the people are very proud, very patriotic, very courageous. I don't think the Afghan revolutionaries will accept any formula that implies renouncing or sacrificing their revolution.

There are all kinds of problems there. I think it's in the interest of all countries in the region to find a solution for that problem. It's in the interest of all the neighboring countries, including the Soviet Union, to find a solution. Everybody must, I believe, observe the principle of respecting Afghanistan's sovereignty and its right to make social changes, to build the political system it deems best, and to have a nonaligned government — since it is a Third World country. This could serve as the basis for a solution to the problems there. It's one of many places with problems.

I think we should work in that direction and not fan the flames of that war and the problems that exist. Rather, we should find some solution that puts an end to the bloodshed and suffering in that country.

That is all I want to say on this question.

Jeffrey M. Elliot: In recent months, King Hussein of Jordan, Palestine Liberation Organization Chairman Yasir Arafat, and President Mubarak of Egypt have put forward a new Middle East peace proposal. Do you believe that this initiative will prove successful in resolving the Arab-Israeli conflict?

Fidel Castro: That's a very complex problem. Among the Palestinians themselves, there are those who disagree with the agreement between the PLO and King Hussein. There has been a lot of mistrust in the entire Arab world ever since the Camp David agreement.

The Arabs considered the Camp David agreement a betrayal, a ploy to divide the Arab world and establish peace under conditions set by the U.S. and Israel. I know this, because I have many dealings with the Arab world. They're very leery of all those formulas.

I'll tell you something. Syria is a key country in that region. After the Camp David agreement, Syria felt betrayed, considering that that agreement had broken the unity between Egypt and Syria, which had existed for a long time.

I believe there is an original sin in the approach to the Middle East conflict — the attempt to impose peace unilaterally and exclude the international community from the search for a solution to that problem. That is, if a solution for the Middle East problem is being sought, discussions should be held with all of the parties and all of the countries. That situation shouldn't be manipulated. I believe that all countries should participate in the solution to the Middle East problem. Any attempt to exclude a country from the solution is unjustifiable. I don't think that the

Camp David approach will resolve the problem. Many years have passed since Camp David, and the problem hasn't yet been solved. So, I really doubt that the present initiative will prove successful. I tell you this sincerely. This is the case for several reasons.

First, there's the position of the United States. It opposes any negotiations with the Palestine Liberation Organization — let's say with the Palestinian liberation movement. Everything stems from the fiction that the PLO doesn't exist, and it is thus ignored. So, in spite of King Hussein's and President Mubarak's efforts, in which Mubarak went to the United States to beg President Reagan to see a Jordanian-PLO delegation, the answer was a prompt and categorical "No." Mubarak was placed in an embarrassing position, as was King Hussein. Arafat was placed in an equally delicate and embarrassing position.

But that's just one aspect of the problem. Not all Palestinians agree with this step that Arafat took on behalf of the PLO. According to my information, a considerable section of the Palestinian movement is against it. There's no unity of views on this issue among the Palestinians themselves.

Moreover, not all the Arab countries agree. There are some Arab countries — important, influential Arab countries — which oppose the agreement.

Furthermore, Israel has expressed its opposition to this kind of agreement.

I don't feel this is the right way to find a peaceful solution to the problems in the Middle East. I don't think this is the way to find a solution. That's my opinion.

I would like to see a solution. War has been raging in that region for many years. It has caused much bloodshed. Peace is needed — but peace without ignoring the rights of any country. Consequently, as long as the problem of a Palestinian state isn't solved, as long as the Palestinian people don't have a state, don't have a homeland — they have been deprived of their homeland — there can be no peaceful solution to the problems in the Middle East.

History repeats itself. However, this time, it's the other way around. Before, it was the Jews who wandered throughout the world, who were discriminated against, massacred, and forced to live in ghettos for centuries. They were the victims of genocide, as in World War II. For a long time, humanity took pains to try to find a solution to that problem, so that the Jews could have a state, a homeland. But, in solving that problem, a terrible injustice was done: the Palestinians were deprived of the land where they had lived for thousands of years. They were banished from their homeland. Now, we are faced with the same problem, but only the other way around — a Palestinian Diaspora.

The Palestinians are very active, very intelligent, very tenacious. No other Arab people has as many teachers, doctors, engineers, or technicians — in proportion to its total population — as the Palestinians. The banishment, the dispersion, has forced them to strive for improvement and knowledge.

Before, it was the Jews who were the victims of pogroms and massacres. Today, it is the Palestinians who are the victims of pogroms and massacres.

Can you think of anything more horrifying than the massacres at Sabra and Shatila, in which thousands of people — including women, children, and the elderly — were brutally murdered? Something similar is happening in South Africa. The South African people — I mean, the black South African people — have been deprived of their land, of their homeland, and are the victims of massacres. That is exactly what is happening to the Palestinians now.

The PLO is charged with terrorism, when what it has done has been to fight for a homeland, for survival, for life. The Palestinians are doing precisely the same things the Jews did when the British troops were stationed in that territory. They've resorted to the same forms of struggle.

When anyone talks about the Middle East, there's one

objective element that cannot be denied: the Palestinians have been deprived of their homeland. They have been scattered throughout the world, deprived of their national rights. Some live in ghettos inside Palestine, subjected to persecution, repression, and all sorts of abuse and injustice. These are real, objective problems. As long as the question of the creation of an independent Palestinian state isn't solved, there will be no solution for the problem.

I think that most of the countries in the international community agree with this. Clearly, serious work will have to be done to find a solution to the problem, so that all the peoples of the region can live in peace and security.

No one should imagine that the revolution is kept in power by force, à la Pinochet. Those methods could not be applied here. If the revolution didn't have the support of the immense majority, it couldn't stay in power.

Mervyn M. Dymally: The United States recently announced its decision to begin its broadcasts on Radio Martí. Do you view this decision as an act of provocation? If so, do you intend to jam the broadcasts?

Fidel Castro: We've never said anything about jamming Radio Martí. Even before it was ever mentioned, we'd already planned to build two powerful medium-wave radio stations and had asked the relevant international agencies for authorization for use of the frequencies. I think it plans to broadcast on one of the frequencies we'd requested. In any case, it's not us but they who've been planning to jam broadcasts.

We haven't started using our stations yet. They've been assembled, but we haven't used them, so as not to heighten tensions and give the United States another pretext for their act of provocation — the creation of that station, so insultingly called José Martí, and the production of subversive programs aimed at Cuba.

José Martí lived in the United States. He learned about the origins of the policy that was developed by the U.S. in this century, its scorn for the peoples of Latin America, its expansionism, and the emergence of U.S. imperialism in the most modern sense of the term. Notice, I haven't used the term very often in this interview. Martí spoke about imperialism; he was deeply concerned about U.S. expansionism in Latin America. He even wrote and said that he knew the monster, for he had lived in its entrails. Several days before his death in 1895 at the battle of Dos Ríos, Martí wrote about what motivated him most deeply: "All I have done so far and will do is for this purpose: to win Cuba's independence in time to keep the United States from expanding through the Antilles and falling with even greater force on our lands of America."

Martí was the most profound political and revolutionary thinker ever born in this hemisphere; he was most deeply Latin American and humanistic — a writer, poet, essayist, journalist, organizer, and leader of the last war of independence in the last Spanish colony in the Americas. He died in action. There is no comparable example.

Martí viewed the U.S. imperial policy as a threat to the development, economies, independence, and unity of the Latin American countries. The use of José Martí's name for a subversive station, aimed against Cuba, is utterly absurd, paradoxical, and indecent.

How absurd that the hero of our independence — to whose efforts our homeland owes so much — is the man whose name the United States intends to use in this campaign. This, in spite of everything the United States did to hinder his patriotic struggle. He was a man who wanted Cuba to be the kind of country it is now — a sovereign and proud nation free of beggars, illiterates, and social injustices. How absurd!

We've never said that we were going to jam that subversive station, a station that will be in the hands of *gusanos*, counterrevolutionaries, traitors. What we have said is that if the U.S. thinks it has the right to broadcast to Cuba to inform the Cuban people — which constitutes radio jamming and political interference — then we feel that we also have the right to broadcast to the people of the United States. We would have the right to inform them about many things that are happening in Latin America, Africa, South Africa, and many other parts of the world, about which they are unaware.

Far from opposing it, we're willing to cooperate, so that Radio Martí can be heard everywhere and so that we can learn the truth — so that, in Martí's name, we can be told the truth. We will even be grateful. We feel it would be desirable to have a debate, a free dissemination of ideas, and the possibility of informing the people of the United States about the horrible things their country is doing all over the world.

I believe it would be good for many of the subjects we've discussed here — the trade and budget deficits, the arms race, and all those magical formulas that have been applied to the U.S. economy and that will have such harsh consequences — to be reported to the people of the United States. Far from thinking about jamming this station, we're in favor of free debate. Do you understand? That's our position. My view is based on the fact that the Cuban people have a much clearer political understanding than the people of the United States. It is the citizens of the U.S. who really need more information in this field.

Nothing has been decided yet. Radio Martí is still nothing but a dream. It hasn't been a fortunate initiative, in any sense. Rather it was more an act of provocation against Cuba. If the United States government had a little more common sense, it wouldn't spend U.S. taxpayer dollars on such a ridiculous scheme. It's a terrible thing to read a news item that says there are 10 million abandoned, poor, and undernourished children in the United States; that children are sleeping in the streets of New York; and that there are homeless children all over the United States. Instead of using this money to save lives and to feed and educate those children, the money of the people of the United States is being spent on stupidities, such as Radio Martí.

Jeffrey M. Elliot: President Reagan has said — and many Americans believe — that you are a ruthless and cruel military dictator, one who rules Cuba with an iron hand. Isn't there some truth to this charge?

Fidel Castro: Well, I'd begin by saying that I'm a unique type of dictator; one who has been subjected here to the oppression, torture, demands, and impositions by a scholar and a legislator from the United States, [*Laughter*] and one who has shown great willingness to discuss any topic openly, frankly, and seriously.

Let's think about that for a moment. A dictator is some-one who makes unilateral, arbitrary decisions; one who is above all institutions and the law, and who is subject to no control other than his own will or whims. If being a dic-tator means making unilateral decisions, governing by de-cree, then you might use that argument to accuse the pope of being a dictator. His ample prerogatives for governing the Vatican and the Roman Catholic church are well known. I don't have such prerogatives. Yet, no one would think of saying that the pope is a dictator.

Reagan can make terrible decisions without consulting anyone. Sometimes he may have to go through the purely formal motions of obtaining the Senate's approval when he appoints an ambassador, but he can order an invasion, such as the one against Grenada, or a dirty war, such as the one against Nicaragua. Reagan can make unilateral deci-sions without consulting anyone. He can even use the codes in the briefcase he always carries to unleash a ther-monuclear war that might mean the end of the human race. If not, why does he have the briefcase? Why does he have the codes, and why does he have an aide with the briefcase? It must be supposed that Reagan could make the decision to unleash a thermonuclear war without consult-ing the Senate or the House of Representatives or his cabinet. And that's something that might mean the end of the human race. Not even the Roman emperors had that kind of power. Reagan appoints ministers, ambassadors, and hundreds — perhaps thousands — of public officials, and he doesn't have to consult anyone. He may ask for ad-vice, but it isn't mandatory.

Now, let's analyze my situation. I don't make unilateral decisions. I play my role as leader within a team. In Cuba, we don't have any institution similar to the presidency of the United States. All basic decisions — all the important decisions — are collectively analyzed, discussed, and adopted. I don't appoint ministers or ambassadors. I don't even appoint the lowliest public servant in the country. We have a system for selecting, analyzing, nominating, and appointing those officials. The president of People's Power cannot make unilateral decisions anywhere: not in the central executive or the municipalities or the provinces. I do, in fact, have some authority; I have influence. But, as I've said, in essence I have one prerogative: I can speak in the Political Bureau, the Central Committee of the Party, the National Assembly, the Council of State, the Council of Ministers, and before the people. That's my authority, and I don't aspire to any other. I don't want or need any other. Those are the conditions in which a political leader in our country must work. I don't think any of these concepts conforms to the idea of a dictator, which comes from the verb *to dictate* — one who is always dictating orders of all kinds. I don't act that way, nor am I empowered to do so. I don't give orders; I reason. I don't govern by decree; nor can I.

During the war, I led an army; in war, it has to be that way. There has to be unilateral responsibility. During World War II, Eisenhower had the power and responsibility to make decisions. But as soon as our movement was organized — long before the attack on the Moncada Garrison on July 26, 1953 — we had collective leadership. Throughout the war, our movement had collective leadership. And, when the war was over, we immediately organized collective leadership to make decisions on the main political issues of the state. These principles have remained unaltered through the years.

I honestly believe that the president of the United States has much greater power and more possibilities for giving orders. Moreover, some of the orders he can give without consulting anyone at all can be very decisive and dramatic. He can, for example, start a thermonuclear war that can wipe out the human race. Nothing could be more monstrously undemocratic. Who, then, is more of a dictator: the president of the United States or me?

As regards concepts of cruelty — you can just imagine — I think that the cruelest people on earth are those who are indifferent to social injustice, discrimination, inequality, exploitation of other human beings, illness, hunger, ignorance, and human suffering — people who don't react when they see a child without shoes, a beggar on the streets, or millions of people going hungry. I really think that people who have spent all their lives struggling against injustice and oppression, serving others, fighting for others, and practicing and preaching solidarity, can't possibly be cruel.

I'd say that what is really cruel is a society — capitalism, for instance — that is not only cruel in itself, but forces men to be cruel. Socialism is just the opposite. By definition, it expresses confidence and faith in man, in solidarity among men, and in the brotherhood of man — not selfishness, ambition, competition, or rivalry. I believe that cruelty is born of selfishness, ambition, inequality, competition, and rivalry among men.

Jeffrey M. Elliot: The U.S. press has reported, on numerous occasions, that Cuba's prisons are filled with a large number of political prisoners — men and women who dared to criticize your regime. And many in the U.S. believe this to be true. Do you deny this charge?

Fidel Castro: There was a time, naturally, when there were a lot of counterrevolutionary prisoners. But there were reasons for that. During the first few years after the triumph of the revolution, when U.S. hostility against our country began — when the CIA began infiltrating weapons, explosives, saboteurs, and established armed gangs in all provinces and dozens of counterrevolutionary organizations, giving them not only material aid but also political and moral support — how could we help having a lot of prisoners? For instance, we captured over 1,200 invaders immediately after the Playa Girón mercenary invasion. Ask those invaders — whom we later returned to the United States in a ship loaded with "heroes" — if any of them were beaten, if any of them were tortured, if any of them were ill-treated.

I'd like to ask a U.S. citizen: What would you have done if 100, 200, 1,000, or — since the United States, at that time, had thirty times as many inhabitants as Cuba — 30,000 U.S. citizens had traveled to Cuba and placed themselves under Cuba's orders? What if we'd organized an expedition against the U.S., and they'd gone back to their country with weapons and bombed, killed, destroyed, and fought in the service of a foreign power? Would you like to tell me what sentence would have been passed on them in the United States? What would they have been called? They would have been called "traitors." Certainly, they would not have been compared to the "founding fathers" or to Lafayette's volunteers. They surely would have been sent to prison, if not shot, as were several U.S. citizens charged with un-American activities soon after the end of the war. They would probably have been sentenced to life imprisonment.

Yet, there you have the mercenaries. How many mercenaries were sent here from the United States? How many were infiltrated? How many were recruited to engage in sabotage, murder, and assassination attempts against the leaders of the revolution? Where are they now? After being imprisoned in Cuba, almost all of them were released before serving their full sentences and are now in the United States.

During the first few years of the revolution, there were indeed many counterrevolutionary prisoners who were later released. The vast majority didn't serve their full sentences. Not only did we set them free, but we also let them go to live in the United States. If they were in the service of the United States, it was only logical that they should live in the United States and be supported by the United States government.

You should keep in mind that, in this struggle against

Cuba, the vast majority of the people who carried out counterrevolutionary activities did so in the service of the United States. Their crimes — considered very serious crimes throughout human history — consisted in acting against their country in the service of a foreign power. It is just like the mercenaries in Nicaragua — who, under the CIA's orders, are waging the U.S.'s dirty war against that small country.

It's true that there were a lot of prisoners during the first few years of the revolution. But, fewer and fewer people were willing to be tools of the United States. Counterrevolutionary activities declined and so did the number of U.S. agents. Many of them are in the United States now, but some are still in Cuba awaiting permission to go to the United States. They consider they're entitled to it; they served the United States and believe the United States has a moral obligation to them. We have given them all the necessary facilities for traveling to the United States.

Our courts hand down verdicts based on laws to punish counterrevolutionary actions. The idea that anyone is punished in our country for professing a belief other than those of the revolution is absolutely ridiculous. There are tens of thousands of people whose political and religious concepts and beliefs differ from those of the revolution. They have full legal guarantees. The idea that anybody is in prison for having ideas that differ from those of the revolution is simply nonsense. No one in our country has ever been punished because he was a dissident or had opinions different from those of the revolution. Our penal code precisely defines those acts for which a citizen may be punished. Some of these laws were adopted prior to the triumph of the revolution, in the liberated territory of the Sierra Maestra, and were applied to punish torturers and other criminals.

We have defended ourselves and will continue to do so. I don't expect that the counterrevolutionaries will put up a statue to me or that our enemies will honor me. I've followed my line all my life — a line of conduct in the revolution, during the war, of absolute respect for individuals' physical integrity. If we had to mete out punishment — even drastic punishment — we meted it out. But, no matter what our enemies may say, or how much they may lie and slander us, the history of the revolution is free of cases of physical abuse or torture. All the citizens in this country, without exception, know this. We waged a hard campaign against these practices throughout the underground struggle and the war. Our cadres, our soldiers, and our people became very aware of and opposed to these methods. I might ask whether any other revolution has maintained the serenity, coolheadedness, firmness, and consistent respect for laws and ethical principles that has typified the Cuban revolution. Not even in the most difficult moments during the war did we depart from those principles!

Why did we triumph in our struggle against the counterrevolution, against the CIA with all its experience? Because our people knew more than the CIA. The CIA worked on the basis of mercenaries, high pay, and accounts in U.S. banks. We worked on the basis of people who had ideals, thoughts, revolutionary fervor, and strong ideological motivations for supporting the revolution and for infiltrating the counterrevolutionary organizations both inside the country and abroad. Our police couldn't use torture, so they developed their intelligence and became very effective in the struggle against elements which lacked sound moral convictions. We often knew more about what they were doing than they did. They might not remember what they had done seven months earlier on a specific day, but we did, because it was on record.

We have defended ourselves with the support of the people and the cooperation of the masses. We've never had to resort to anything illegal — to force, torture, or crime. Throughout the entire history of the revolution, no one can point to a single case of torture, murder, or disappearance, which are common, everyday occurrences in the rest of Latin America. Another thing: never has a demonstration been broken up by the police! Never in twenty-six years has a policeman used tear gas, beaten a citizen during a demonstration, or used trained dogs against the people. Never has a demonstration here been repressed by the army or the police — something that happens every day everywhere else in Latin America and in the United States itself.

Every so often I see dogs and policemen in action in the United States. I see prostrate people being violently and humiliatingly stepped upon. Something else: I frequently see demonstrations being broken up everywhere. How strange that this revolution has never used a policeman or a soldier or tear gas or a dog against the people! Why not? Because the people support it; the people defend it. All the people are soldiers; all the people are policemen. All the people defend the revolution.

Injustice, violence, torture, disappearance, and murder — those things happen in countries whose governments are against the people, whose governments have to defend themselves against the people — in Argentina under the military dictatorship, in Chile, El Salvador, and elsewhere — with repressive forces and death squads trained by the United States. You see, they need those procedures to defend themselves against the people. When the people themselves are the revolution, when it is the people who resolutely defend the revolution, you may rest assured there'll be no need for violence or injustice to defend it. Ours is the only government in this hemisphere — I can state this proudly — that has never used a policeman or a soldier against the people, never inflicted any bodily harm upon an individual, and never resorted to political assassination or disappearances.

Look what happened in Santo Domingo when the people's protest against the International Monetary Fund was repressed — 50 dead and 300 wounded, according to the official figures, or more than 100 and 400 people respectively, according to absolutely truthful and credible people and organizations. That sort of thing happens every day in the rest of Latin America and the Caribbean. Our government has also, for many years, been the only one constituted and defended by the people. How is it that we have been able to stand firm against all of the U.S.'s ploys, acts of subversion, and threats? Because of the people and their support. That's the essential thing, and the United States should realize this.

Pinochet's methods can't be used to defend a revolution. Cuba's army is the only one in Latin America that's composed of all the people: workers, peasants, students, men and women from the cities and the countryside. Nearly all university students are combatants, members of our defense units. Our country is the only one whose defense and whose armed forces are composed of all the people. It cannot be a repressive army or a repressive regime, because it's based on the people's support and consent. It doesn't have to resort to any illegal actions, violations, or injustices to defend itself. Furthermore, no people can repress itself.

We are defending ourselves and will continue to do so. If anyone engages in counterrevolutionary actions that are punishable under the law, we punish him. We don't let ourselves be pressured or blackmailed; we don't let ourselves be influenced by calumny, lies, or any other kind of direct or indirect pressure.

This is the line, the policy, that the revolution has followed. I trust that history will record this. This is what I say to that unfortunate misconception which many U.S. citizens have.

I'm sure that every day they see things there that are never seen here — acts of violence against people. They see many things that simply can't happen here. Here, no one has ever seen — nor ever will — the murder of a civil rights champion, such as Martin Luther King, Jr. Actions such as this have never occurred here; yet, we don't go around bragging about the revolution's humanitarian spirit and respect for human rights.

Mervyn M. Dymally: In your view, are you loved by the Cuban people? If so, why?

Fidel Castro: I think that the people have a feeling of familiarity, confidence, and respect. It's a very close relationship, very close.

Several factors have contributed to this. Our people don't look on leaders as distant, untouchable figures. I remember how it used to be. In the past, if someone knew a legislator or a mayor, he looked on him as a great figure. It was unusual — amazing — to meet a head of state. That is, leaders, officials, were viewed as distant beings. With the revolution, that phenomenon was ended. The people don't look on anyone as distant, as a demigod.

I think it's a family relationship. The people look on me as a neighbor, as one more person. They aren't overwhelmed by positions, by public figures. No one even calls me "Castro." There is familiarity, of course, but there is also respect — confidence, familiarity, and respect. I believe that the element of confidence is based, among other things, upon the fact that we've never lied to the people. The people know it — and not only the people who are in Cuba. The Cubans in Miami also know it. These people don't have any feelings of familiarity or affection. But they do have confidence and that has been evidenced many times. If we tell them they can come, they come. That has been demonstrated more than once — first, during the Camarioca and, later, during the famous Mariel episode. If they ask us: "Can we pick up our relatives?" and we say "Yes," they all come — even if they're our worst enemies, even if they have serious unfinished business with the revolution, even if they are terrorists. They know that they have our word, that there'll be no tricks, betrayal, or entrapment. We're like the Arab of the desert who welcomes his enemy in his tent and doesn't even look to see which direction he takes when he leaves. The people who are in Miami — say what they might — know the rules of the revolution. They also know that when the revolution gives its word, it keeps it.

Of course, this is based on the fact that we have never told a lie. Never! This tradition dates back to the war. Throughout the war, all the information we released on the fighting — the number of casualties, the munitions captured — was all strictly accurate. We didn't add one single bullet or rifle. That same tradition, initiated by the first rebel column, was followed by the rest. These columns would arrive at the central part of the island, or the northern part of Oriente Province, and establish a radio station. We knew that when they reported an action, that report was accurate. That is, not even war justifies a lie or the exaggeration of a victory. This has been a very important element in our revolution. Whenever surrender conditions were negotiated, the enemy soldiers and officers of any encircled unit were absolutely confident that those conditions would be strictly observed.

Then there is another objective element which explains our relationship with the people. Who forms the immense majority of our population? First and foremost, the working people. The workers and the peasants, the manual and intellectual workers, have many reasons to support the revolution. Women, who constitute half of the population — be they workers or housewives — the country's black population, and the students and young people in general also have many reasons to support the revolution.

The vast majority of our professionals have been trained since the revolution. We have 255,000 teachers and professors, over 90 percent of them trained by the revolution. On the average, we have one teacher for every eleven students in this country, including university professors and primary school teachers. Of course, a primary school teacher might have twenty students, while a university professor has much fewer. The number of doctors is already 20,500.

In September 1985, 2,436 new doctors will graduate. Freshman enrollment in the medical school is 5,500 annually. The students are selected according to their vocational aptitude and academic performance. There are medical schools in all fourteen provinces. There is not a single corner of the country without a school. All children between the ages of six and twelve attend school — except for reasons of health. That goes for more than 90 percent of the children between the ages of six and sixteen. Forty thousand children with visual, hearing, or other types of impairments attend special schools. There is not one young person denied the opportunity of entering the educational system due to a lack of high schools or technical schools. Medical services cover the entire country. Job opportunities have been created for all. Culture and sports have developed. The population is organized; every sector has its organization.

Women organized themselves during the early years to fight against all forms of discrimination and inequality, and to work in the revolution for those measures that would guarantee their right to employment, social and political equality, and quality health care and education for their children. Today, women make up 53.8 percent of the country's technical force and 37 percent of the labor force — the largest figure in Latin America — and they get equal pay. Women have an outstanding participation in our homeland's defense. Hundreds of thousands of them are part of the territorial troop units or participate in various activities of the regular armed forces. The Federation of Cuban Women comprises 3,100,000 women over the age of sixteen.

Every worker has social security and a guaranteed retirement pension. All production and service workers are, naturally, organized. Nearly three million workers are members of trade unions. All the country's farmers belong to farm associations. All the country's neighbors are organized by area of residence — men and women, workers, housewives, retired persons, students, and young people. Together, they make up over 80 percent of Cuba's adult population. These mass organizations are a gigantic force. All university and high school students are organized and, through their associations and federations, are intensely active. They directly take up a wide range of issues of interest to them as young people, students, and revolutionaries. The children are also organized. Here, everyone has his or her organization. They have hundreds of Explorers' camps, Pioneer "palaces," vacation centers, and they themselves organize and take charge of an important part of their own activities.

Moreover, no farmer pays rent for the acquisition or holding of land, and the vast majority of the urban population doesn't pay rent; they're already home owners. There are no taxes on housing or on landownership.

To understand the people's support for the revolution — their confidence, affection, and respect for their leaders — you must take into account the work of the revolution. The whole spectrum of social, political, and material problems — problems of all sorts — has been solved for a population always neglected by its rulers and which still remembers the past. Parents, relatives, and grandparents all remember the past and hand down their experiences to the new generations. A new state has been formed, with totally new cadres — almost all of humble origin. This includes the armed forces, with all its officers coming from the most humble families, the sons and daughters of blue-collar workers, small farmers, white-collar workers, and technicians. Progress has been made in a country where over a half million boarding school students receive clothing, room and board, and medical and dental care free of charge. And where more than half a million children also receive free school lunches and where workers have a minimum of a ninth grade education. There are 200,000 university students in a population of 10 million — more than 50 percent of them workers. Schoolteachers who, for instance, are studying for a bachelor's degree in primary education, have all the conditions to combine work and study, and are paid their full wages during the last years in order to study full time.

Workers have all the facilities they need to further their education, and practically all of them are enrolled in educational programs. To this we can add the results achieved in the drive for public health. Life expectancy is already equal to that of the United States — seventy-three to seventy-four years. Infant mortality is only three points higher than that of the United States — the United States, twelve; Cuba, fifteen. There is one doctor for every 485 inhabitants, over 35,000 nurses, and a similar number of intermediate-level health technicians. Just these two sectors alone — education and public health — account for 600,000 workers, of whom over 350,000 are professors, doctors, teachers, and intermediate-level technicians.

Cuba's nutritional levels are among the highest in Latin America. We have an average daily intake of eighty grams of protein and 3,000 calories — without the agricultural resources of Argentina or of other Latin American countries. We don't have a single beggar. There's not one single abandoned child in the streets — not one lost or missing child. There's no prostitution, gambling, or drugs. Alcoholism is practically nonexistent; alcoholic beverages have rather steep prices. Fortunately, we don't have that kind of problem, which is very serious in many countries. We have eradicated many diseases and have developed effective and systematic preventive medicine. For example, the early detection of cancer in women — breast cancer, cancer of the cervix — is one of the activities carried out by the women's and the mass organizations, thus contributing to saving many lives each year.

I'm trying to point out factors that explain why there is strong and sound support for the revolution. Just compare all this with what Cuba had before the revolution! Don't you think that the people appreciate all this?

We rank first among all Third World countries with regard to education and have a higher standing than several industrialized countries. We are first among all Third World countries with regard to public health — with higher rates than those of several industrialized countries — and are rapidly catching up with those that rank first in the world. For example, our infant mortality rate places us among the top fifteen. Moreover, we have thirty pediatric hospitals and each one of them boasts an intensive care unit with the most sophisticated equipment. Any child in this country receives, totally free of charge, the same care available to a child in the United States at the Mayo Clinic, with a specialized staff and sophisticated equipment.

The homes of 85 percent of the population have electricity; only families living in remote areas of the countryside lack electricity. Almost all households with electricity have television sets. Almost all cities have water and sewage systems, and sports facilities. Around 17,800 physical education and sports teachers have graduated since the revolution, close to 3,000 of whom have bachelor's degrees from the Higher Institute for Sports and Physical Education. There are tens of thousands of artistic and cultural groups for children. Workers have also created tens of thousands of amateur artistic and cultural groups. Almost everyone participates in sports.

Now, I'm going to point out several other facts. Thousands of libraries have been opened up all over the country. Every municipality has movie houses, museums, libraries — a minimum of ten cultural institutions, what we call "cultural modules."

There's no possible comparison between Cuba's situation and that of any other Third World country. For example, we're already beginning to develop a new medical service, in addition to the whole network of polyclinics and specialized, clinical-surgical hospitals. We're placing a doctor in every school, a doctor in every factory, a doctor in the community who will care for around 120 families — a male or female doctor and a nurse. We just recently began this service, and over 200 newly graduated doctors are already working in that program. Next year, we'll have 500 more, and, within the next fifteen years, 25,000 doctors will be working in this program. This service doesn't exist in any other country — capitalist or socialist. We call these doctors — who work directly in the community — "family doctors." They have the medical records of every resident. They're in the community. They know of all the risk cases: heart, blood pressure, diabetes, respiratory problems, and so on. They not only have an office in the community, but they also visit those risk cases periodically at their homes. These doctors have the overweight out jogging and the elderly walking. In the next fifteen years, we'll graduate 50,000 doctors. Today, we already have 1,500 doctors working abroad, and, in the next three five-year periods, we'll have about 10,000 doctors on internationalist missions, according to estimates.

I've mentioned a series of factors which explain why the population identifies with the process, why it supports the revolution, and acknowledges what has been done by the revolution. Yet, I've not covered them all. Other cities in the country have been transformed. There are universities, cultural institutions, and factories in all the provinces. To these, powerful moral factors must be added: patriotism, a sense of justice, equality, solidarity, and fraternity among human beings. There's a recognition of the dignity inherent in all the men and women who constitute the people the revolution embodies. They possess future dreams, new ideas and values, an internationalist spirit, and the universal and historical sense of transformation. "Man cannot live by bread alone," and neither can material and social progress justify the power of a revolution.

No one should imagine that the revolution is kept in power by force, à la Pinochet. Those methods could not be applied here. If the revolution didn't have the support of the immense majority, it couldn't stay in power.

Our army and our police are not trained in repression, because the entire population is part of the armed forces. In the days of absolute monarchies, the king could say: "I am the state." Today, any citizen of this country can say: "I am the state," because he or she is an essential part of the country's defense forces, ensuring law and order and sharing in many productive, political, and social responsibilities. The phenomenon of the revolution cannot be understood if you don't realize that it is sustained in power by the support of the people and not by force.

I repeat, if one day the revolution did not have the support of the overwhelming majority of the people, it could not endure. This revolution cannot be sustained in power by force.

Revolutionary values, revolutionary integrity, dedication to the revolution, are the traits I first look for in a person.

Mervyn M. Dymally: Do you have many close friends? If so, what do you look for in a friend? Do friendships play a significant role in your life?

Fidel Castro: I have many friends who are not Cuban, who I've met through different relationships, mainly political. I've established relationships with outstanding personalities: doctors, writers, filmmakers, scientists — friends from abroad. Now, my friends in the revolution are all the revolutionary comrades, all those who work with me, all those who hold important responsibilities in the state. We have this type of friendly relationship. I have friendly relationships with those who ride with me in my car — the security personnel and those who accompany me wherever I go — those who go fishing with me, and those who cook and otherwise look after me. They're also my friends.

I don't really have what you might call a circle of close friends. For me, a circle of friends is a very broad concept. I don't have the habit of always meeting with the same group of eight or ten friends. I visit one friend one day; another another day. With some, I talk more because of work relations. That's logical. However, I've tried to avoid — since it's not a good practice, from the viewpoint of my responsibilities — to cultivate just one group of friends whom I might see, for instance, every Sunday. I have many friends in my work relations. I stick to this; other comrades may act differently. As a rule, there are groups of friends who meet more frequently. I generally don't do this, because soon there is a group of people who are believed to be more influential, because they are your personal friends and can convey firm opinions to you. So, I've really tried to avoid that practice.

Fortunately, all these friends are in the sphere of revolutionary activities. It cannot be conceived in any other way. I speak with a lot of people — scientists, doctors, professors, journalists, economists, athletes — every chance I get, because I know many of them personally. But the field of interesting and valuable persons is so extensive, that one does not have to take refuge exclusively in only one group of friends. Revolutionary values, revolutionary integrity, dedication to the revolution, are the traits I first look for in order to become fond of a person; then comes personality, talent, a series of things. But for me, what is essential, first of all, are the revolutionary traits of a friend. I view all revolutionary compatriots as comrades and friends.

Jeffrey M. Elliot: Are your friends — both personal and political — able to challenge you, question you, take issue with you, or are they intimidated by your role or position?

Fidel Castro: I'll start by telling you this: there's a large group of comrades holding responsibilities in the state, in the leadership of the party, and they have an important position, practically as important as mine. Now, individual characteristics have something to do with this. As a rule, almost all of them come to me with great familiarity to raise any concern, problem, or question. That's the rule. There may be exceptions — someone who comes to me as if he didn't want to inconvenience me or as if he didn't like stating a problem. But, I repeat, that's an exception. In those cases, I make it a point to make communication easier. Everybody has the same possibilities. In general, my relations with comrades are excellent. But now that you've asked me, there are two or three people for whom I'm always a headache. [*Smiles*]

For instance, Comrade Chomy [José M. Miyar Barrueco], who's right here, heads these offices. I have three: one for Council of State matters; a second for party matters; and a third staffed by a team of comrades who work directly with me on many matters. It's a team of about twenty men and women — selected for their ability, experience, modesty, and seriousness. They visit many places all over the country: factories, hospitals, schools, sugar mills, agricultural enterprises. Since I don't have much of a chance to move around, there are comrades who are constantly going to all those places on my behalf. They meet with the management and the leaders of the party, trade unions, and communist youth. They visit the workers' cafeterias, talk with them, help them solve problems, and, when necessary, coordinate things with other industries and work centers. Nothing escapes their attention, and they have a well-earned prestige. I have an office for this.

But the one who has the roughest time with me is Comrade Chomy, and he can testify to it. He's the one with whom I argue the most and to whom I complain most about things: if there are too many papers; if among the papers there was an important one, and, instead of putting it aside, he left it with the rest, so that even if it was terribly important, three days went by before I took a look at it. He has the unrewarding duty of showing me the list of people I have to see or who ask for a meeting. Since for me, for one reason or another, almost everyone is important — and there's not enough time — we can't be happy. And so, he's the one who has the toughest time with me. After all, I have to have someone to whom I can complain and grumble.

Next in the list comes the comrade who runs the party office; he also has a difficult time, but at least there's less daily contact. Besides these two, no one else has a tough time with me, no one else. [*Grins*]

Mervyn M. Dymally: Do you view yourself as emotionally driven? Are you obsessed by your work? If so, do you find it difficult to relax?

Fidel Castro: Let me explain, because they're two different things. Emotion is one thing. There's emotion in everything: even in a sporting event, in a boxing match, in baseball — in a game or match between the U.S. and Cuba — in an assembly, a congress there are emotions. One gets emotional even talking to you, under your cross-examination. I speak to you, we talk. With visitors, emotion is indeed present. Emotion is always present as is interest in thousands of things. That's one thing; obsession is another thing.

I've had an obsession these days: You! [*Laughter*] Every time I remembered that you were here since Friday; every time I remembered I hadn't finished other things and had to meet with you — that I had promised we were going to start on such and such a day, and then I said the next day because I was really tired. Then the congressman returned at 2:30 in the morning, after an important congressional session, and I called off last night's session because I was tired, and they told me the professor is making a lot of fuss about it. [*Smiles*] I said we were going to meet at 6:00 p.m. and time was passing, but I was doing something else. Some ambassadors asked for meetings at the last moment. By the end of the afternoon, I was in an awful quandary. If I don't meet with the ambassadors, I might spoil international relations or perhaps they want to inform me of something important. Other comrades are urgently asking to see me — and so you have become an obsession with me.

This doesn't usually happen. I'm rather used to keeping my word and trying to get things done. But this time, I had unfinished work — materials to be sent. The Mexican journalist is still waiting here for part of his material. Last night and this morning, I had to work on that, going over the transcripts. And you were waiting.

I only very rarely become obsessive or feel in a quandary. But, as a rule, if I really didn't have a sense of humor, if I didn't joke with others and even with myself, if I weren't able to let go, I wouldn't have been able to handle the job. I also ask myself the same questions. How's my blood pressure? How's my heart doing? How have I been able to stand it for so many years?

I meet people who I immediately know are going to die young. I see them all worked up, bitter, tense. But that's not my case. I think that something that has been a great help in this is that I'm able to let go, that I have a sense of humor — that I can see the light side, the funny side, and even the ridiculous side of things that happen. That has helped me to hold on. But I can also grab a book and forget about you until tomorrow. [Grins] So, you see, I can do it; I can move around, change activities. I can let go perfectly well. That's the only way you can stand up under this type of intense work for so many years. I also believe that exercise and moderate eating habits have also helped. And why not? Nature and luck have also helped.

Jeffrey M. Elliot: Unlike many leaders, you do much of your important work late at night. How are you able to maintain your concentration, what with the long hours you expend each day?

Fidel Castro: Don't think I always work like this. The fact is, I'm always trying to get on a normal work schedule. I'm constantly getting back on schedule, then constantly getting off of it. Let me give you an example. During the days you've been here, I've been getting up early — 7:00 a.m. every day and sometimes even at 6:30 a.m. That's the reason we haven't been working late at night. And that's why at midnight, I've said: "We'll leave that for tomorrow."

I've slept very little these last few days, but last night I slept seven hours. Today, I got up around 8:00 a.m. Since I talked my way out of seeing you yesterday, and we scheduled an interview for today with the pretext that Dymally — who returned in the early morning — should be present, I left early. I even had the luxury of doing different things: I went to see visitors who were about to leave. We talked, but by 1:00 a.m., I was sleeping. By 8:00

a.m. the next day, I was up and about. Naturally, I went to work immediately: read papers, did all sorts of things, until I had lunch. I continued working almost all evening. I didn't come to the office on account of you, [Smiles] because of the slavery I've been subjected to these past days. But — I repeat — this doesn't happen every day. I hope to settle things by the beginning of next week. I worked a lot today, especially since I was trying to keep my word to the Mexican journalist, who only had part of the transcribed and revised material.

On a day like today, the schedule goes out the window. It gets out of control. This is frequently the case, particularly when visitors are leaving the next day. I'm going to tell you how it works. A lot of visitors come to Cuba: foreign ministers, party representatives, a great many people who demand and deserve my attention. I'm well aware that all governments are pleased to see that their representatives and envoys receive as much attention as possible. The smaller the country, the more attention I try to give its delegation. When they arrive, a program is made for them: the first day, such and such activities, meetings with the heads of the various bodies; next, a visit to Santiago de Cuba; then, rest at Varadero. Then I ask for the visitor; I want to see the visitor today or tomorrow, at such and such an hour. But they tell me: "No, he's in Santiago de Cuba." "No, he's in Varadero." "No, he's in Pinar del Río." So, when I want to see him, he's not around. But also, I don't want to tie myself down with too many engagements either; there are many who visit our country. In many cases, I prefer to remain free to see them, if possible, without any commitment. The exceptions are those who are my personal guests or to whom I've made previous commitments.

If I were to set an exact date and hour for each visitor who asked for an interview through Comrade Chomy, through the party, through the Ministry of Foreign Affairs, through the executive committee, through all channels, I'd be tied up all the time. There are a great number of requests for interviews. Besides, there are the unforeseen interviews, because all of a sudden an envoy arrives from one place or another with whom I have to meet. I like to keep my word and be punctual. I dislike meetings which are purely protocol. They are a waste of time. I prefer to talk about interesting things with visitors. And I dislike keeping an eye on the clock. I also dislike interfering with their schedule. As a rule, I tell their hosts: "Make up the schedule; I only want to know where they are and when they're free." This has, of course, its inconveniences.

Many times, after they've made the tour — and they're back in Havana — they tell me: "Minister so-and-so is leaving tomorrow; guest so-and-so is leaving tomorrow." And then, as a rule, in those cases I am forced at times to meet with them at night, often very late. I agree. But no one upsets my life as much as interviewers and journalists do.

Of course, I guess it's just habit, training oneself to put up with so many hours of work. Like the long-distance runners, I always have a second wind, or a third wind.

Mervyn M. Dymally: Do you ever give thought to marriage, a family, settling down? Are these important priorities?

Fidel Castro: Let me tell you something: I won't talk about this, [*Smiles*] or only a little.

I've always been allergic to social columns; to publicity about the private lives of public men. I believe that's part of the few intimacies that one has. When you were speaking about the fishbowl, the ivory tower — one has very few things that escape the constant scrutiny you were speaking about. And one of them is one's private life. That's why I maintain discretion — until one day. Someday, the things you're interested in will be known, but not with my cooperation. I can tell you that everything is perfectly well with my private life — no problems.

Jeffrey M. Elliot: You're known as a superb communicator. Does public speaking come easily to you? Was this a born gift or something you've had to develop over the years?

Fidel Castro: I'm going to tell you something that people might not believe. I tell people that I have stage fright. I mean, whenever I'm going to speak in public, I go through a moment of tension. For instance, in huge rallies, at the closing session of a party congress, an international event, a medical or technical congress, or a congress of one of the mass organizations: women's, workers', etc. On all of these occasions, when I have to make a closing speech — when I have to broach complex subjects — I have a moment of tension. What I mean is, I don't enjoy making speeches. I take it more as a duty, a delicate task, a goal to be met, a message, an idea, a feeling that has to be conveyed. I feel the burden of the responsibility for what I have to say there. I can't imagine speaking to anyone if I don't have something to say. I don't like to repeat speeches. I don't even like to repeat phrases. I find it boring, or at least it bores me.

When I have to participate in a session of the National Assembly — a normal session, lasting several days — or at a workers', women's, farmers', or youth congress, where I have to speak on numerous occasions — as we are doing here, discussing these problems — where there are 500, 800, or 1,000 people present, or in smaller meetings of the Central Committee, I do so more normally. When I have to speak frequently, I feel more relaxed. That's more or less my reaction to that type of activity. But I'm always greatly confident, determined, and certain that I can do my job when I'm at the rostrum. I make sure that I'm well informed on the topic. On each of those occasions, I have the basic ideas — you might say, a small mental script of the essential ideas — and more or less the order in which I'm going to present them. But I work out and develop the ideas — the words, phrases, and forms of expression — during the speech itself.

People prefer that to when I bring a written speech. There are times when one must have a written speech: international events, the United Nations, the Nonaligned Movement. The mere fact that what you say has to be translated into several languages demands that you have a written speech if you want to ensure a modicum of fidelity in the translation and spare the nerves of the simultaneous interpreters, whose work I admire. Sometimes, on very important historical occasions which are commemorated in the country or at other appearances where one must use a great deal of facts and figures, then I write the speech. But for some reason, people like it better when the speeches are not written. It seems to me that they like to see the man's struggle — his efforts to elaborate ideas.

Sometimes when the audience knows that someone is making a great mental effort to work out his ideas, they can almost guess what's coming, and they follow closely. They prefer that to a written speech, which is always colder and the fruit of abstract inspiration. The public likes to see the birth of arguments and ideas. This has led me, on certain occasions, to dispense with the written speech and retain a great amount of data — on education, public health, the economy, or other topics — in my head. Sometimes when I speak, I have to keep 80 to 100 facts in my head.

I remember an international pediatrics congress that was held recently. I was to speak at the opening of the congress and present data on infant mortality and various diseases at different stages of the revolution. I had to mention the death rates for measles, respiratory problems, tetanus, and gastroenteritis by year — exact figures, including fractions. It was an infinite amount of data. I had to retain it all in my head. How? It's very simple. If you give me a telephone number, I'll forget it — that is, unless I have a special reason. However, if you give me a figure dealing with economics, I hear it or read it once and I don't forget. A figure on public health, education, economic development, or even scientific data in which I have special interest, I don't forget. I read it once, sometimes twice. Perhaps I repeat it to myself, with the paper nearby to see if I omit something, and then again without paper. Then I retain it all. It doesn't require a special effort when I'm interested in and have a command of the subject. If I had to retain data on a topic with which I wasn't familiar, I would surely forget it. Another thing: I never try to explain something that I myself don't fully understand or haven't mastered.

Some things are harder to retain. I'll give you an example: when you have to mention the factors that have led to a given result — maybe fifteen, sixteen, or seventeen of them — and give them in the correct order, that's more difficult to manage mentally than figures. If you want to avoid taking a written speech and you have to make an analysis of that sort and mention seventeen factors — as, for example, at a scientific congress — then you have to make a greater effort. But in that case, I resort to the basic ideas of the topic, with which I'm generally familiar. I think about them, try to retain them, and repeat them in my mind in the order I deem most appropriate. That eliminates the written speech and having to carry around papers with data. It also saves much needed time. But I confess that it takes a bit more effort, especially when there are several sets of factors. Then you have to have them in a clear order of priorities, every set and every element in each set — and always in association with the main ideas. But when I master the topic, when it interests me, when I have thought it over, I can do it perfectly. If I didn't master the topic, if it didn't interest me deeply, it would be impossible to do it.

Nevertheless, if it's a very solemn occasion — though I don't like to — I write the speech or dictate it. Generally, I draft it in tiny handwriting in a notebook, either during the day, in the evening, or at dawn. Once I've finished my normal activities, I will dictate it to the stenographers. The job of revising is sometimes more difficult, because words are changed or omitted in the transcription. Sometimes small details slip by me when I scan the copies. If, by chance, one has slipped by, I discover it when I'm on the rostrum delivering the written speech. That never fails.

The only advantage in writing out the speech is that the tension disappears and you can sleep easier the night before. You've got it all done — it's just a matter of standing up and reading it. You don't have to give birth to ideas. When you don't have it written, there's the tension of ideas racing in your mind and the pressure of the test. It's like before an exam or a battle. I generally have the main ideas, the essential ones — five or six basic ideas — and a central objective of the presentation. Then I develop the ideas while I speak, and new ideas and arguments occur to me. The ideas flow more easily when the speech is political, historical, revolutionary.

I have learned that contact with the public — the influence of the public — is the best source of inspiration. Ideas and arguments suddenly take form that didn't occur to you the day before or many days before. When you're in direct contact with the public, nothing is artificial, nothing is abstract. You get better ideas; words are more persuasive, more convincing. I'm also convinced of one more thing: when you speak to a specialized audience — doctors, economists, professors — if you take a written speech, they always assume it was written at the Ministry of Public Health or some other agency, and that you're merely repeating what's been drafted. Sometimes experts in given fields are reluctant to concede that politicians can know anything about anything. They're amazed when they discover that a layman knows something about their specialty; they're even flattered. As you can see, I've revealed some of my trade secrets.

Mervyn M. Dymally: As you grow older, do you find yourself more obsessed with age, with your own mortality?

Fidel Castro: Fifteen or twenty years ago I worried about it more than I do now. I was more worried about the passing of the years and approaching old age. It's undeniable that nature has placed some fabulous balance and compensation mechanisms in people. The more the years go by, the less I worry about death and old age. Isn't that curious?

What could have contributed to this? I would say that twenty years ago, I thought I needed a lot of time to fulfill a mission, to complete a task. As time passes, you start to get the feeling that a large part of the task that was your lot in life has already been fulfilled and that what you have accomplished lives on. Then you are less anxious about health, age, and death. Why? Because the achievements remain. You've done the work you set out to do; the job that had to be done, is done. Likewise, your vocations or aptitudes have been put to use. So you can rest easier. You have greater tranquility. I can tell you that I am not at all bothered by health, old age, or death.

The only pressure I might feel is that you must make the best use of your time and do as much as you can. Since you have less time, you have to make maximum use of it, especially because it coincides with the period in life when you are more experienced and can be more useful.

Mervyn M. Dymally: Clearly, you can't live forever.

Fidel Castro: I have been reminded of it more than once tonight: old age, the passing years, death. [*Laughter*] What do you want to know?

Mervyn M. Dymally: What plans do you have, if any, for the succession of power?

Fidel Castro: Well, of course, I don't have any plans for dying.

Jeffrey M. Elliot: And for a successor?

Fidel Castro: Plans for that? Yes.

I'll tell you this: since the beginning of the revolution, since the very first year — particularly when we realized that the CIA had plans to shorten my life — we suggested the nomination of another comrade, Raúl Castro, second secretary of the party, who would immediately assume leadership. In my opinion, the comrade chosen is the most capable, due to his experience and revolutionary merits. He played a very important role in the Moncada attack. He was with us in prison, in exile, on the expedition, and in the mountains. He was the one who led the group of four armed men who, after meeting up with me again, collected the first seven weapons and later formed the twelve-man group that resumed fighting. He was the one who led the first column to leave the Sierra Maestra and establish the second eastern front, and he is the man with the greatest authority, experience, and merit to replace me. I think that immediately after that happened they would have to look for his deputy.

I believe that the cadre who are to assume responsibilities cannot be improvised. They must be chosen from among the most capable. That must be one of the party's main tasks. There must be one, two, or three comrades to really guarantee continuity in leadership of the revolutionary process. They must be people with great authority and prestige before the people and of proven capabilities.

I'm going to tell you something: I know revolutionaries. There are many comrades here — all old guerrilla fighters — in very responsible positions. But, some of them still have much of the rebel in them. They take orders from one or two — generally two — old guerrilla leaders, but they don't readily accept criticism from someone else or anybody else giving them orders. That, of course, is the case with the older cadre of the revolution. Young people have other ideas about discipline.

I have stated, before the Central Committee, the party, everywhere, that the founders — or whatever you wish to call them — of a revolution, those who began a revolution, really have great authority. They have an authority of their own, born of their participation from the very beginning.

They have the prestige that pioneers always have. Those who participated throughout the struggle have this.

During these years, tens of thousands of qualified cadre have emerged, even more qualified than we were from a technical viewpoint. They have greater political and theoretical qualifications and a greater sense of discipline. Although there might have been one or two people, or a small group of people, with many merits among the thousands or tens of thousands of cadre, this will not be the case in the future. There will be tens of thousands of new cadres with merits — people who have been working all these years for the revolution, who have fulfilled internationalist civilian or military missions, who have acquired great merit in the revolution. There are tens of thousands of people who have, more or less, the same merits.

In the future, of course, no one leader will have authority per se — that is, authority as a result of having been one of the pioneers in this revolutionary process. He won't have this personal authority. So, there is only one solution — I'm thinking twenty years down the road, or maybe sooner, depending on how long the old founders of the revolution live and on their physical and mental capacity to lead the country. The authority of future leaders, aside from their capacity and revolutionary merits — which are similar to those of many others — must be given by the institution. The party is the one to give it, because if you're going to choose one person, when there are hundreds of capable people — people with merits, with a revolutionary background — then only the party can give to those leaders the great authority they need. Do you see what I mean? That's the principle I insist upon. At the last meeting of the Central Committee, we also talked about this question: how the party is the only one that can give authority.

These are some reflections I made on these problems: all revolutionaries must be self-critically vigilant. They must have humility, modesty. They should never allow themselves to be blinded by the glitter of power. We insist a lot on this, because it's the only way of ensuring leadership quality and unity. Only institutions can solve this problem.

Despite the great demand and need for worthy cadres that the state and party have, I do my best to choose outstanding cadre from the youth organizations to work with me. They are part of a work team — about which I spoke to you earlier. They constantly visit factories, schools, hospitals, agricultural enterprises, and other centers related to production and services. They know what the workers think, what the managers think, and they coordinate activities among the various bodies and help solve problems. They acquire a lot of information on, and overall knowledge of, problems. They visit sugar mills, universities, research centers, art groups, theatrical troupes, the National Symphony Orchestra, the National Ballet, the Operatic Ensemble, and the National Dance Ensemble. Every year, for one reason or another, these people visit all the factories and production or service centers in the country to check economic plans, raw material savings campaigns, and the quality of services.

The team is made up of about twenty comrades, male and female. Among them, there are several technicians, engineers, and other professionals. Their activities are highly useful and allow them to gain great experience.

Sometimes, one of these cadre is requested for a specific party or government responsibility. If I can't refuse, I try to replace them with new people; say, an outstanding engineer, another professional who works at the grass-roots level, or a valuable party, youth, or mass organization cadre. Capacity, dedication, enthusiasm, integrity, and modesty are required of them.

In our country, there's a strict system for the promotion and training of cadre — in the party, the Young Communist League, and the mass organizations. I think that we must constantly bring the young people into the party and the government. We have a great many of them, a fabulous human potential for this. We would be truly shortsighted if we didn't devote special attention to these questions. But I don't think we have or will have any difficulties in guaranteeing the continuity of the policy of the revolution.

Jeffrey M. Elliot: If you were to step down from power tomorrow, how would you like to be remembered? What would you like historians to say about you?

Fidel Castro: This time I haven't died, right? [*Smiles*]

Let me say this: If tomorrow I were to resign all my functions, there'd have to be a truly convincing reason for the people to understand it. It would have to be logical, natural, and justifiable. I couldn't just say: "I'm going to drop these activities because I'm bored with the job or because I want to lead a private life." It would be difficult to explain and difficult for the people to understand. The people have also been instilled with the idea that one must do everything possible, that one must give top priority, to all revolutionary obligations.

For example, if I were to say that I would like to retire — that I want to write, anything of the sort — it is most likely that the people wouldn't understand it. The effect would be negative. It would set a bad example, because the people have been instilled with the concept of giving their utmost, their maximum, if necessary, of sacrificing their personal interests. Doing something that runs contrary to this would not be well understood. It would be rather disappointing to the people.

Well, what would happen? Let's say that my absence were justified. If it could be explained, then everyone would understand it perfectly well. I believe the people would be certain that whoever succeeded me would be quite capable of discharging those duties. This would not disrupt the revolution in any way. There might be some sadness, but the people would adjust perfectly.

I don't have the slightest doubt, though, that I can still

be useful and make further contributions to the revolution. There are still some things which need a little time to mature. I believe the opinion of people — their recognition of the role I've played and my efforts in the revolution — would be truly high. This in no way means that everything has been perfect, free of error, or anything of the sort. But I'm quite sure that there'd be a high opinion of my services. I'm absolutely certain. I haven't the slightest doubt about it.

Jeffrey M. Elliot: The Castro beard and revolutionary jacket have long been symbols of revolutionary consciousness. Are you fully aware of your impact on international dress and style?

Fidel Castro: As for the origin of the beard, it was simply the lack of razor blades during the guerrilla war. Everyone grew a beard and let their hair grow long. Gradually, these became first an element of identification — the guerrilla fighter's identification card — and later a symbol. In the beginning, it had a great deal of influence. I now see a lot of people wearing beards, who come from different countries. But I don't know if that's still a result of the Cuban revolution.

As for the uniform, the Chinese, who made their revolution before we did, might have had a greater influence on fashion than we have. There's no reason for us to think that we're the sole promoters of beards, long hair, and simple attire.

Jeffrey M. Elliot: Given your demanding schedule, do you have much time for reading? If so, what you do read? Are your tastes eclectic?

Fidel Castro: That's something that has varied with time, even over the years. Of course, when I was younger, purely literary works and novels, for example, interested me more than they do now. Obviously, a good novel is pleasant reading, recreational reading. So, I read many novels. I remember perfectly that during the twenty-two months I spent in prison, I read fiction and other literature. There weren't enough books there for the fifteen or sixteen hours a day that I read. Although prison doesn't exactly have the best possible atmosphere for pleasurable reading, it helped a great deal to make time fly and made you forget you were in prison. I read classical literary, economic, historical, and political works. But throughout my life, I've usually preferred historical works, as well as biographies, nature books, and narratives. For instance, I was impressed and fascinated by Humboldt's books and descriptions of his travels in Cuba and other countries. I also enjoyed Darwin's book on his voyage on the *Beagle* around South America, the Pacific, and the Galápagos Islands, where he conceived the theory of evolution.

I've read practically all of Stefan Zweig's biographies. I was very attracted to them. I also read many biographies by Emil Ludwig, though I liked Zweig's better, because of his imagination and his ability to recreate historical periods, characters' lives, customs, and environment. I like historical narratives, even when they're blended with fiction. I consider *The Book of Marco Polo* — a volume of over 800 pages — a fabulous narrative that mixes fact and fiction. I also like many books that were written in ancient times, such as Plutarch's *Parallel Lives* and Suetonius's *Lives of the Caesars*. Books on real or fictional history interest me very much.

I also like historical novels. I know how much fiction they contain, but they teach and illustrate. I like books that blend history, biography, nature, and fiction. One example is a work on Orellana's trip on the Amazon. In terms of recent books, I particularly recall Haley's *Roots*, a wonderful reconstruction of the human tragedy that was slavery — though its idyllic ending was not quite to my liking, bearing in mind the injustices that existed and still exist in the world.

Among the books on nature that I like most are the ones

edited by *Life*; its collections on science; outer space; the atom; energy; the human body; life; the formation of forests, soils, fauna, and flora in North America after the glaciers; the studies of the Amazon basin; the descriptions of Mount Everest and the Himalayas, the East Indies, and other parts of the world. What interests me is the absolutely scientific approach: no concessions in explaining the geological evolution of the earth, the evolution of human life, the explanation of natural phenomena. And it's all expressed in understandable language. There's no doubt that the authors were well chosen.

I also like certain scientific books — that is, books on plants and crops, soils, the laws of natural evolution, biology, genetics, genetic engineering and biotechnology, medicine, and scientific research in general. I'm also very much interested in that kind of scientific literature, as well as in some books on economics, especially when they contain an explanation of some important phenomena concerning the role of banks, international finance, mineral resources and raw materials, and the problems of transnational corporations. I'm very interested in books that present contemporary problems and phenomena. Of course, I try to read everything that falls into my hands that contains information on the problems that affect Third World economic development.

Lately, in particular, I've been reading fewer novels. Although good novels are enlightening and educational, due to my lack of time, I've come to regard novels as purely recreational. Of course, there are some very interesting novels of special value; those I read. But the others I mentioned, even aside from the interest I have in them, give me knowledge and information on many important topics we're constantly dealing with.

I've read many memoirs — from Churchill's, which are quite unwieldy, interesting, with a lot of historical data, to de Gaulle's — which reflect the thoughts, styles, and ideas of outstanding contemporary personalities. I've also read numerous books on World War II and the main events which took place then. I've read most of the books dealing with the actions of that war, both by Western and Soviet writers and military men. I've read practically all those books — memoirs, narratives, particularly those about military actions. I've always been very interested in that kind of literature.

It goes without saying that I've been an inveterate reader of the *Communist Manifesto* and of Marx's, Engels's, and Lenin's classic works. I've read many works on the October revolution and that historic process. At one time, I was also a voracious reader of anything and everything on the French revolution. I believe that those books exerted the same influence on me as did the books of chivalry on the noble squire, Alonso Quixano. I haven't mentioned Cuba, but it is to be imagined that I've read everything I could lay my hands on about our history and our wars of independence.

Mervyn M. Dymally: Do you read many books in English?

Fidel Castro: I can read some books in English, particularly technical and political books. Novels have a richer, more varied vocabulary, full of subtleties and nuances — I don't read them in English. Logically, I prefer to read everything in Spanish.

I haven't mentioned Russian literature. Works such as Sholokhov's, which describe the early years of the Bolshevik revolution and the problems with the peasants and the Cossacks, have always interested me very much. By the way, during the previous stage — when I was in prison — I read all of Dostoyevski's and other Russian authors' novels. Years later, I read Tolstoy. *War and Peace* is, in my view, one of the most fabulous literary works ever written because of the way in which it recreates history, customs, and dialogue as well as its moral, philosophical, and human content. I'm deeply grateful for that type of novel.

As a student, I greatly enjoyed reading Hugo's *Les Misé-rables;* while in solitary confinement, the inspiring and satisfying volumes of Rolland's *Jean Christophe.* I encountered many of the classics during those hazardous years of my life.

Once in a while, I delve into the roots of the language. I recently reread Cervantes's *Don Quixote,* one of the most extraordinary works ever written. If it weren't for the long narrative passages it contains, which make it somewhat boring at times, I would read some excerpt from it every day.

I've also read all of Hemingway's works — some of them more than once. I'm really sorry he didn't write more. I've also read most of García Márquez's novels, stories, historical works, and newspaper articles. Since we are friends, I'll dispense with the praise.

But in recent years I've devoted my attention to technical, scientific, economic, and political books. Some of them are written by journalists — actually, very brilliant people with a great ability to discuss complex problems intelligibly. Of course, a new book always appears — memoirs of contemporary figures and literary works of special interest for any number of reasons.

I'd say that it's really mind-boggling to think of the enormous number of quality publications that are printed every year and the contradiction between the desire to read all of them and the real possibility of reading very few.

Mervyn M. Dymally: What newspapers and magazines do you read regularly?

Fidel Castro: Very rapidly, I read *Granma* and *Juventud Rebelde.* These are two of the Cuban papers I read.

Now, as I've already explained, every day I receive quite a large number of international wires from all the agencies: European, U.S., Cuban, and socialist. I receive, maybe, 200 wires every day. Fewer arrive on Monday, because usually nothing important happens on Sunday — politicians take the day off. Wires become more numerous on Tuesday, by the middle of the week. By the end of the week, the amount of information is enormous — whole dispatches, not summaries. Summaries are always very poor. I don't like that method. I'd rather read the index and choose those wires in which I'm most interested. I always read about economic topics, of course: what the World Bank, the other banks, and other economic organizations have had to say. I also read all the scientific and medical items; the news items that have to do with Cuba; the news coming from the United States; and everything that has to do with major problems of world interest. The news items are divided by area. I choose those wires I'm most interested in.

Many of these are unimportant, but the ones I'm interested in, I read in full. Then I really get an idea — not just from one source but from all possible sources, quite up to the minute — of all the various problems that are developing in the world. This may include hunger in Ethiopia, Central American issues, the Latin American debt, a strike in Bolivia, or U.S. congressional debates.

This morning, I learned that the U.S. Congress passed the MX missile by a six-vote margin. I read about Reagan's press interviews; Shultz's statements; what was said in China, the Soviet Union, and Geneva; and what everyone said about the infinite number of current issues — catastrophes, earthquakes, volcanic eruptions, ecological crises, and the political situation in Spain, France, and the German Democratic Republic. In short, there was quite a lot of information. My main sources of information, you see, are the international wire services.

For Cuban problems, I turn to the newspapers: news about sports, the activities of the mass organizations, and the economy. Those are the topics about which I read most. I think the youth paper is more lively, because the party newspaper must print communiqués, news, and many other things — sometimes obligation and protocol make it necessary to print too much material.

For example, as a rule, the paper inserts an item every time I meet with a delegation. Sometimes, even four such items are published in one day. The next day I learn from the papers that I had met with three of those delegations the previous day. It's lucky that most of the people I meet with don't fall into this protocol category. Those things take up a lot of news space.

Unfortunately, I can't watch much television, and I very seldom listen to the radio due to time constraints. Sometimes, when there's a very interesting program on television, or some sports event I can't catch, I have it taped so that I can watch it later. Only in the summer — when I take short holidays — am I able to watch television. Significant sports competitions, the Olympic Games in which we participate — that kind of event — I always follow attentively.

I also have the usual sources of information. The party prepares bulletins on various topics; the Ministry of the Interior also issues information; and the intelligence institutions also send their information. There are certain news dispatches from various sources that I read every day, because they are short, easy to read, and necessary.

Besides these, there are a large number of wires sent by our embassies and an enormous number of papers from all over the world that Comrade Chomy collects for me every day and presents me with when I call it a day. I don't always read them within twenty-four hours, and sometimes they pile up. That's how I found out that you were coming. All the contacts of our Interests Section in Washington and other topics are channeled that way. I also receive the most incredible and diverse domestic items: such and such a family wrote about a given problem, or one about the most pressing problems that the families of former guerrillas or other Cuban families face. Comrade Chomy screens all such information and passes it on to me.

I'm quite up-to-date as to what is happening inside the country and abroad. Actually, if anything happened on a sugar plantation, if there were some difficulties in a factory, if there were problems with a given line of production — anything that affects our economy — I'm sure to have the bad luck to find out about it. [*Smiles*] There's a report on everything of interest: if something happens in Oriente, if such and such a school has a problem. There are many people who send out papers, reports. Sometimes, I get a list with a summary of all those things, and I'm kept informed of what's happening. I get that every day — to make me happy or spoil my day.

Jeffrey M. Elliot: Earlier in the interview, you mentioned *Don Quixote*. Is there anything about Don Quixote, the character, with which you especially identify?

Fidel Castro: Well, I think revolutionaries are the closest thing to Don Quixote, particularly in his desire for justice. It's that spirit of the knight errant, of righting wrongs everywhere, of fighting against giants.

It has been said that *Don Quixote* was written to ridicule the romances of chivalry. In my view, it was written very ingeniously, with a good pretext. In fact, I think it's one of the most marvelous exaltations of man's dreams and idealism. Above all, it is interesting. We have two characters: Sancho, with his feet on the ground, who looks at problems and gives advice. A model of caution, he considers all worldly details. And then there's Don Quixote, always dreaming about a noble cause to defend.

I believe that a revolutionary would identify with Don Quixote. Why not? Many times revolutionaries are called "Quixotes." Don Quixote's madness and the madness of the revolutionaries are similar; their spirit is similar. [*Laughter*] I believe it's an honor for a revolutionary to be compared to Don Quixote. I like that character very much. I'm sure that he wouldn't have hesitated to face the giant of the North.

Mervyn M. Dymally: What are your tastes in music, art,

and theater? Do you enjoy such cultural activities?

Fidel Castro: I like music very much — that is, as recreation, as relaxation. I'm specifically referring to classical music. I also like Latin American and Spanish folk music. I also like protest songs, hymns, marches, and some romantic songs. Any type of music can be pleasing to me if it isn't too loud or monotonous.

I get very little chance to go to the theater. I've been interested in some plays, especially those that deal with our country — plays related to the life of the small farmer, the revolutionary struggle, the counterrevolution, and the types of conflicts, contradictions, and problems generated by a revolution.

What's happening with the theater? The new media — cinema and television — have, in fact, reduced the influence of the theater. Our country has good theatrical groups, and I've suggested that television should be used more to present plays to the public. A magnificent group of artists, a good play in a good theater, can be seen by a thousand people in one night; maybe 20,000 to 30,000 in a month. If you use television, 6 million people could see the play at the same time. It seems to me that some of the contradictions that have emerged must be overcome and these media combined.

Television has had a huge impact on our country. Ten years ago, we had a project to build movie houses. Today, we have too many of them. We've had to face the problem of what to do with them, what type of cultural or theatrical or other activities could be performed there. We have to transform the movie houses into social centers, and show films as part of the overall activity. Television has started to replace other forms of entertainment, not only the theater but also the cinema. The party is shortly going to look at the problems of the cultural sphere. We're going to analyze these matters in depth.

We have more than fifty art schools in our country and one higher institute of art. I believe we've advanced in these fields. Cuba's ballet is certainly among the finest in the world. It has world stature. Another top quality ballet company has been created in the province of Camagüey. The visual arts are developing quite a bit. A Latin American visual arts biennial was recently held, in which a large number of young Cuban artists participated.

We are trying to promote these cultural activities. But, the fact is, I have had very little time for theater and music. As for the ballet, we hold a ballet festival every year. I generally go on closing night, at which the best troupes and ballet dancers of the festival perform. I have plenty of contact — direct and indirect — with these art groups, and we give them the maximum possible support. But my possibilities for enjoying these activities are very limited.

Mervyn M. Dymally: Finally, what about the Olympic Games? Does Cuba intend to send a team to the 1988 Olympic Games in Korea?

Fidel Castro: There's been no decision in this regard. We've raised with the Olympic Committee the need to share the Olympic Games between the two parts of the Korean territory. If the Olympic Games are held in a country where a bloody war was waged — a war in which hundreds of thousands of people from many nations died, which caused destruction, and which inflicted deep wounds on the Korean people — then those Olympic Games, as they have been planned, will be sectarian. Rather than creating unity, they will divide. Rather than healing the wounds, they will infect them. They won't serve the purposes of peace and cooperation among the peoples. For this reason, we've proposed to Mr. Samaranch, president of the International Olympic Committee, that the games be shared between the two parts of the Korean territory as the only possible solution.

We must not forget the problems that cropped up in Los Angeles. There wasn't any security in Los Angeles. It would be difficult to argue that there will be any in Seoul under a repressive, bloody regime — a regime that is an exact replica of Pinochet's Chile, or rather the one after which Pinochet patterned his. You know about the horrible violations of civil rights that are being committed there. You know that South Korea is crawling with U.S. bases and U.S. soldiers, besides being the property of U.S. transnational corporations. To insist on holding the Olympic Games as planned, totally disregarding these historical realities, will, I believe, create a very serious problem for the Olympic movement. This will be the case no matter how much whistle-stopping Samaranch may do in Europe, in the socialist countries, and everywhere else or how many trips multimillionaire Vázquez Raña may take in his swanky private jet to Africa and the rest of the Third World, after having sold the 1987 Pan American Games to Indianapolis for $25 million, thus depriving Cuba of that right. Despite their optimism, it won't be easy for them to extricate the Olympic movement from the enormous trap in which it has been placed.

Let's wait and see the reaction of the Third World, of the Nonaligned Movement, of the socialist countries — which didn't attend the Los Angeles Games, because of the lack of security — and what China will do. Keep in mind, a hundred thousand sons of the Chinese people died there, fighting against the U.S. troops that invaded what is now the Democratic People's Republic of Korea.

Frankly, I believe that the Olympic Games, as planned, are going to create some very embarrassing situations, morally speaking, for many countries — and not just the socialist countries but many Third World countries as well.

I've talked with several Third World leaders; they like our proposal. They feel it is fair and view it as the only possible solution to the problem that has been created. I believe it's the only thing that would avoid serious difficulties and a possible setback for the Olympic movement.

The Olympic movement was created in the time of colonialism. So far, the Olympic Games have served to parade the rich, industrialized countries' wealth, good nutritional standards, and excellent technical capacities. How many medals have been won by athletes from the Third World, from those countries that lack sports facilities, physical education and sports instructors, and proper nutrition for the children and young people from whose ranks the athletes must come? How many medals have they won in past Olympic Games, and how many have the United States and the other industrialized countries won? On many occasions, those events serve to foster scorn for the countries of the Third World — the countries of Asia, Africa, and Latin America. They are viewed as so backward, so impotent, so incapable, so intellectually stunted that they hardly ever win a medal in the Olympics. Every four years, the Olympic Games measure the inferiority of the Indians, blacks, yellows, and mestizos and the superiority of white society, even though it is U.S. Blacks who win most of the medals for the rich, white, industrialized society of the United States.

Samaranch has requested that the United Nations support the Olympic movement. I agree completely, though I don't think we see eye to eye on concepts, aims, and intentions. I feel — and have for a long time — that the United Nations should not only take an interest but also a hand in sports, as it does in science, education, culture, health, industrial development, and economic relations among countries.

I definitely favor the United Nations having an agency, like UNESCO, UNICEF, WHO, or UNDP, that will advance, promote, and support sports and physical education. Sports and physical education are vital activities for the health, education, recreation, and well-being of man. Participating in sports and physical exercise could do more for humanity than a million doctors. Today, physical exercise is used as therapy to prolong life and to combat many ailments. Sports and regular exercise educate, discipline, develop the will, and prepare human beings for life and work. I think I owe it to sports that I was able to hold up under the difficult conditions of life in the mountains and then tolerate twenty-six years of intensive political work, without a heart attack or hypertension. Yet, over 4 billion people in the world have only a vague idea of what sports are.

National and international sports organizations could continue to operate independently of the United Nations agency to which I'm referring. Even the reformed Olympic movement could go on existing — but with truly democratic rules, whereby all countries would be represented by delegates elected in each of them — under the guidance of the United Nations. Even the Church was once reformed; why not the Olympic movement?

It might be preferable for this proposed United Nations agency to handle the Olympics. It's not a matter of the United Nations supporting the International Olympic Committee, but of the United Nations reorganizing and directing the Olympic movement.

The resources from sports events should be used to help the Third World countries — especially those with the least resources — to develop sports, so that they, too, will have the right to host the Olympic Games. So far, the Olympic Games have been held only in rich countries, with the sole exception of the Mexico games. Who has won all the medals in the Olympic Games? How has the $200 million collected at the Los Angeles games been used? It has been said that the money will be invested in sports facilities in the State of California. It is there, as well as in the rest of the United States, where the greatest number of sports facilities already exist. Why isn't the money invested in a poor Latin American country, such as Bolivia or Ecuador, or in Central America? Why isn't it invested in Burkina Faso, Ethiopia, Mozambique, or other African countries? Why isn't it invested in helping to build sports facilities in poor countries in Asia and other Third World countries? The granting of $200 million to the richest state in the rich-

est country of the world shows the weaknesses and anachronistic ideas of the Olympic Committee, which is attempting to bring professional sports into the Olympics. This
grant amounts to pillage and outright robbery. It is morally
indefensible, since the proceeds of the Olympic Games are
the result of the efforts of athletes from all countries. Without them, there would be no Olympic Games or any proceeds. They say they're going to return part of the expenses that the Third World athletes incurred at Los
Angeles. That's as insulting an act of charity as the little
presents which Vázquez Raña takes the Third World
sports leaders in his private airplane.

The Olympic movement was created in the time of colonialism, and many of its methods, its style, and its ideas
are rooted in old ideas dating back to colonial times. We
really aren't colonies any more. We don't need counts,
marquesses, and millionaires to tell us what to do in the
field of sports. That's why I favor the United Nations taking a hand.

In our countries, we have more than enough physical
and mental potential for sports; what we don't have is
socioeconomic development, sports facilities, and food for
the vast masses of the population — and, at times, even for
the athletes.

I believe the same thing is happening in sports as in the
Third World countries' economies. Already, the big European cities — London, Barcelona, and Paris, the former colonial capitals — are squabbling over which of them will
host the 1992 Olympic Games, and where the few athletes
from the neocolonial countries are going to play their role
as also-rans. What chance does Ethiopia, Mozambique,
Angola, the Congo, the Republic of Guinea, Tanzania,
Zambia, Zimbabwe, or any other African country have of
hosting the Olympic Games? What chance does Ecuador,
Peru, Guyana, Nicaragua, or any other of the more than a
hundred Third World countries have of hosting the Olympic Games? When will one of these countries be able to

host them? That's why I say again that the United Nations should step in. I think that if this problem is discussed, many interesting things will be brought out.

In short, I feel the same about this concept of the Olympic Games as I do about the relations between the rich industrialized world and the Third World.

Earlier, you asked me if Cuba is going to send a team to the 1988 games. There's plenty of time to reflect on this question and discuss it with our friends in the Third World and socialist countries. We have much to say about this.

If the Olympic movement is to be saved, they will have to avoid the catastrophe of Seoul and share the Olympic Games. The Democratic People's Republic of Korea would be willing. I think this would help to save the Olympic movement and then transform it, because it can't keep going from one crisis to another: a crisis in Moscow, a crisis in Los Angeles, and certainly a crisis, the way things are going, in Seoul. That crisis — which is institutional, not situational — must be overcome. Once this is done, the Olympic movement must be transformed — reformed — because it can't go on like that. Some tiny European countries that have few athletes have two representatives on the International Olympic Committee, while other countries that are more important in terms of sports have none. This organization doesn't represent different countries; rather, it is a self-serving, oligarchic, autarkic institution that names its representatives from the countries of the world.

Since you asked, I will tell you frankly that this is an institution that was created and organized along lines dating from the past century — from the Middle Ages, if you wish — like the orders of chivalry during the Crusades. It's being manipulated by the big Western economic powers. Politics is mixed up in this. I think the most serious issue is Seoul. Where did the idea come from? Who inspired it? How could they make such an absurd decision?

Fidel Castro

Fidel Castro Ruz was born in Birán, in the former province of Oriente, on August 13, 1926. Born into a wealthy landowning family, he received his primary education in a rural school and later attended private boarding schools in Santiago de Cuba and Havana. In September 1945, he entered the School of Law of the University of Havana, where he received his Ph.D. in law and an additional degree in international law.

While at the university, he joined a student action group, the Unión Insurreccional Revolucionaria [Revolutionary Insurrectional Union]. He was a founding member of the Partido del Pueblo Cubana [Cuban People's Party] in 1947 and became a leader of its left wing. That same year, he joined an aborted armed expedition that had planned the overthrow of the Trujillo dictatorship in Santo Domingo. As a student leader, Castro traveled to Venezuela, Panama, and Colombia to help organize a Latin American anti-imperialist student congress. While in Bogotá, he participated in the popular uprising of April 1948.

After Fulgencio Batista's coup d'etat of March 10, 1952, Castro began to map out plans for what he believed would be an inevitable armed struggle against the self-proclaimed president. He organized and led an unsuccessful attack against the Moncada army barracks on July 26, 1953. He was captured, tried, and imprisoned. His famous speech during the trial, "History Will Absolve Me," became the program of the July 26th Movement. Sentenced to fifteen years in prison on the infamous Isle of Pines, he was released on May 15, 1955, as a result of intense public clamor.

In July 1955, Castro left Cuba for Mexico and later visited the United States, where he attempted to raise funds for launching an armed struggle in Cuba. On December 2, 1956, along with eighty-one other guerrillas, including his brother Raúl, Che Guevara, Camilo Cienfuegos, and Juan Almeida, Castro approached the Cuban coast aboard the yacht *Granma*. After an initial setback, the guerrillas, the nucleus of what was to become the Rebel Army, were able to reorganize their forces and successfully pursue the struggle in the Sierra Maestra. For two years, Castro directed the operations of the Rebel Army, participating in all of the major operations and battles along the first front.

On January 1, 1959, Batista fled and the war came to an end. Castro and the Rebel Army arrived triumphantly in Havana on January 8. Castro became commander in chief of all air, sea, and land forces. On February 13, he was named prime minister of the Revolutionary Government, and on May 17, president of the National Institute of Agrarian Reform.

He served as prime minister until December 1976, when he became president of the Council of State and the Council of Ministers. He has been first secretary of the Central Committee of the Communist Party since its founding in 1965.

Dr. Jeffrey M. Elliot is Professor of Political Science at North Carolina Central University, as well as a free-lance journalist. A prodigious writer, he has authored over 50 books and 500 articles, reviews, and interviews. His work has appeared in more than 250 publications, both in the United States and abroad. He has interviewed nationally and internationally known figures in world affairs, American politics, litera-  ture and the arts, science and technology, and sports and entertainment. In 1985, Shaw University awarded Dr. Elliot an honorary Doctor of Letters degree. In 1986, California State University, San Bernardino, established the Jeffrey M. Elliot collection. Dr. Elliot serves as a Distinguished Advisor on Foreign Affairs to Congressman Dymally.

Congressman Mervyn M. Dymally (D-Calif.) has held numerous elective offices, including lieutenant governor of California, state senator, and state assemblyman. As a member of the U.S. House of Representatives, he serves on the Foreign Affairs Committee (and Asian and Pacific Affairs and Western Affairs Sub-  committees) and the Education and Labor Committee. He is Chairman of the Congressional Caucus for Science and Technology. A recognized authority in international relations, Congressman Dymally (who holds a Ph.D. in human behavior), has traveled to every continent and met with dozens of world leaders, including

Fidel Castro, King Hussein, Rajiv Gandhi, Shimon Peres, Daniel Ortega, and Yasir Arafat. A former teacher and magazine publisher (*The Black Politician*), Congressman Dymally presently serves as president of the Caribbean-American Research Institute. An expert in Caribbean affairs, science and technology, and educational opportunity, he has authored or co-authored six books and dozens of articles.

Index

Also Available from Pathfinder Press

Nicaragua: The Sandinista People's Revolution
Speeches by Sandinista Leaders
More than forty speeches and documents from 1982-84, including the FSLN's platform in the 1984 Nicaraguan elections, the "Plan of Struggle." Nicaraguan President Daniel Ortega, Vice President Sergio Ramirez, Tomás Borge, Jaime Wheelock, Victor Tirado, Bayardo Arce, and others discuss subjects such as U.S. destabilization and aggression, women's rights, the history of the FSLN, and problems of the Atlantic Coast and the Miskito Indians. 430 pages, $8.95.

Maurice Bishop Speaks
The Grenada Revolution 1979-83
These speeches by the late Prime Minister Maurice Bishop of Grenada explain the revolution that unfolded in that Caribbean nation between 1979 and 1983. Bishop discusses the gains the revolution had made and had planned in health care and social services, the constant threat of U.S. intervention, and the importance of the airport construction project to Grenada's development. Published as appendices are the statements by the Cuban government and Fidel Castro on the October 1983 Grenada events — the murder of Bishop and the subsequent U.S. invasion. 400 pages, $7.95.

Order from
Pathfinder Press
410 West Street
New York, N.Y. 10014

Also available from distributors listed on page iv.